FLYING HIGH

STORIES OF THE BALTIMORE RAVENS

Jamison Hensley

SPORTS
PUBLISHING

Sports Publishing books may be purchased in bulk at special discounts for sales promotion, corporate gifts, fund-raising, or educational purposes. Special editions can also be created to specifications. For details, contact the Special Sales Department, Sports Publishing, 307 West 36th Street, 11th Floor, New York, NY 10018 or sportspubbooks@skyhorsepublishing.com.

Sports Publishing® is a registered trademark of Skyhorse Publishing, Inc.®, a Delaware corporation.

Visit our website at www.sportspubbooks.com.

10 9 8 7 6 5 4 3 2 1

Library of Congress Cataloging-in-Publication Data is available on file.

Cover Design by Owen Corrigan
Cover Photo Credit AP Images

ISBN: 978-1-61321-658-3
Ebook ISBN: 978-1-61321-682-8

Printed in the United States of America

For my son Jackson,
I hope these pages make you proud one day

CONTENTS

ACKNOWLEDGMENTS

When I was first approached about this project, I was reluctant to say yes.

I had never written a book, and I honestly didn't have the time considering my son was six months old. In my mind, I was the last person that should take on such a project. Thankfully, my wife Abby thought otherwise.

She is my best friend, confidant, and in football terms, the best cheerleader anyone could ever hope to have. Her faith in me became my driving force, and her advice shaped the chapters that lie ahead.

This book would never have been written without Abby.

Thanks to my parents, Junior and Patricia, for their sacrifices and support over the years.

Thanks to ESPN for allowing me to pursue this endeavor.

Lastly, thanks to all of the current and former Ravens. Your tales and generosity created the foundation of this book. Time is a valued commodity in the NFL, and I was humbled by the minutes, and often hours, given to me.

My first interview was with public relations guru Kevin Byrne, the best storyteller in the business. My last was with Ravens owner Steve Bisciotti, whose talks will always rank as the most memorable of my career. Along the way, the interviews with players and decision-makers were nostalgic, humorous, and insightful.

The only way I can repay you all is with a book that properly honors the hard work of champions.

INTRODUCTION

To understand the history of the Ravens, you must first go back to that chilly February afternoon in 2013, when a crowd of 200,000-plus people from across Maryland poured into the heart of Baltimore.

Two days after the Ravens defeated the San Francisco 49ers in the Super Bowl to sit atop the football world, fans dressed in purple stood shoulder to shoulder along the city's streets for the victory parade, and they filled M&T Bank Stadium to capacity for a celebration party no one could have envisioned only two decades earlier.

"I don't know how many more times we can do this before Baltimore loses that chip on its shoulder," Ravens owner Steve Bisciotti told the crowd. "I hope it doesn't ever happen."

The "chip" on Baltimore's collective shoulder is the result of being used and abused by the NFL after the Colts left town in 1984. Teams like the then–St. Louis Cardinals and Tampa Bay Buccaneers used the city as a bargaining chip to get better deals and stadiums elsewhere. The NFL turned down Baltimore's profitable expansion bid in 1993 in favor of Carolina and Jacksonville.

NFL commissioner Paul Tagliabue even had the audacity to tell Baltimore to give up hope of getting a new football team and to use that money to build a museum, a statement that still boils the blood of many fans.

"The NFL is never going to give Baltimore a franchise," then-Gov. William Donald Schaefer angrily said at the time. "The only way we're going to get a team is if we steal one. Just like the Colts were stolen from us."

After 12 long years without football, Baltimore was forced to do just that—lure an NFL team from another city. On February 9, 1996, the Cleveland Browns moved to Baltimore, leaving their legacy behind. The city was left with a football team that had no identity and no history.

Owner Art Modell's original choice for a name was Bulldogs, in honor of the Canton, Ohio, team that helped start the NFL. Team executive vice president David Modell envisioned a team called the Americans. And former Colts quarterback Johnny Unitas preferred to keep the equine theme with Mustangs.

As the result of a fan poll, the name ended up being a ghostly bird immortalized by Edgar Allen Poe, whose grave sits a long football toss from where the team now plays.

The Ravens became the perfect marriage of blue-collar players and a blue-collar city. The franchise won its first Super Bowl in 2000 with a roll-up-their-sleeves defense. Baltimore found itself on top of the football world again in 2012 with an "Average Joe" quarterback.

Coaches, players, and even owners have changed for the Ravens. What has remained is a team that embraces its underdog roots.

This work is a collection of stories about those who turned a displaced and disparaged franchise into one of the model organizations in the NFL that still proudly carries a chip on its shoulder.

Establishing
A Foundation (1996–98)

Chapter 1

FORMING AN IDENTITY

Art Modell

The Ravens exist because of one person—Art Modell.

He brought football and joyful Sundays back to Baltimore. But it came at a personal price.

"I'll never forget the sadness on his face as we did the deal," said John Moag, the former head of the Maryland Stadium Authority that helped bring the Browns to Baltimore. "The pain of leaving Cleveland was immeasurable."

The only son of a Brooklyn, New York, middle-class couple, Modell had his heart broken when his beloved Dodgers baseball team relocated to Los Angeles.

Modell felt that same betrayal decades later when Cleveland taxpayers built new playing facilities for Major League Baseball's Indians and the National Basketball Association's Cavaliers. Prospects for a football stadium dimmed as those two projects ran over budget and an unrelated bond crisis gripped the county.

The Browns were left to play in 65-year-old Cleveland Municipal Stadium, which often had no running water and housed portable toilets in the Dawg Pound due to a lack of functional restrooms. The stadium was more than inadequate. It was dangerous. Chunks of concrete were falling off the stadium's facade, and team officials always prayed no one would be in the building the next time it happened.

"I didn't get into this business to go bankrupt," Modell said at the time. "I'm in it to win, and I can't continue to make the best effort to win in Cleveland with the current stadium situation."

Modell's biggest regret, in hindsight, was never challenging the politicians. He didn't want to be another Robert Irsay or Bill Bidwill, who threatened communities with ultimatums.

Modell believed it was inappropriate to talk about losing millions of dollars on a sports franchise when steelworkers were going broke in nearby Youngstown, Ohio.

"I always thought it odd that he didn't want to threaten them, he just moved," said Kevin Byrne, Ravens vice president of public relations and confidant of Modell for over 30 years. "It's like you're going through a divorce and you never have the arguments. You just say, 'I don't like it and I'm leaving it today.' That's kind of what happened."

That divorce turned the once well-respected member of the Cleveland community into a villain in his adopted hometown of 35 years.

"Yeah, it hurt," Modell said. "They [the politicians] lied to me. They sold me out. They took for granted that Art Modell would never move the team."

Modell never set foot in that city again, but nothing would have made him happier than to be invited back to the Cleveland area, specifically the Hall of Fame in Canton, Ohio.

The NFL was Modell's life, and he was just as much a fabric of it.

Modell didn't just *know* about Vince Lombardi. He worked *alongside* the legendary coach to complete the league's first collective bargaining agreement.

He didn't just *reap the profits* from the partnership of the league and television. It was Modell and late commissioner Pete Rozelle who *negotiated* the first contracts that are now the standard and help separate the NFL from other sports.

Moving his franchise to Baltimore has overshadowed these accomplishments with Hall of Fame voters, even though there are four owners in the Hall of Fame who have relocated their franchises: Dan Reeves (Rams), Al Davis (Raiders), Lamar Hunt (Chiefs), and George Preston Marshall (Redskins).

"Someone once said to me, 'If you can't tell the history of the game of football without mentioning this person, then they are without a doubt, a Hall of Famer,'" offensive tackle Jonathan Ogden said in his Hall of Fame speech. "Well, there is no way that you can tell the history of pro football without mentioning Art Modell."

The players' loyalty stems from their strong bond with the affable owner. One of the first conversations players had after being drafted or signed was with Modell. His warmth and charisma made you feel like you were his best friend after a five-minute chat. He spoke to his players about their personal lives after practice, and he even knew the practice squad players by name.

In 2000, when defensive tackle Larry Webster violated the league's substance-abuse policy for a fourth time, Modell welcomed him back on the team. When a member of defensive end Michael McCrary's family needed medical attention, Modell sent out a chartered jet and made sure that person was seen by some of the nation's top doctors.

And, in 2000, when Ravens linebacker Ray Lewis was charged with murder, it was Modell who flew down to Atlanta to be a character witness at his bail hearing.

"The whole football team is like a family," Modell's late wife, Pat, once said.

That family was there when Modell fell gravely ill just before the start of the 2012 season. Lewis, Ed Reed, Haloti Ngata, and Terrell Suggs all visited the hospital to say goodbye.

Ravens coach John Harbaugh kissed Modell on the cheek. "I told him how much I loved him, how much the players loved him," Harbaugh later said. "I assured him he would see the best of us Monday night."

Modell never saw the Ravens open the 2012 season, passing away four days before that Monday night kickoff. To honor Modell that night, Ray Lewis put "A.M." on the strips of black under each of his eyes.

The memory of the Ravens founder was felt throughout the championship campaign. There was a black "Art" patch on the uniform of every player that season, just above the heart.

"It brings a tear to our eyes today, seeing images," said David Modell, the former team president and Art's son. "The image that was on the front page of *The [Baltimore] Sun* paper of Joe Flacco holding up the trophy after the game, and Art was all over that. We felt pretty good about that."

Ozzie Newsome

Modell agreed to leave the Browns' name, colors, and record book in Cleveland. He just wasn't going to head to Baltimore without future Hall of Fame tight end Ozzie Newsome.

The invitation to follow Modell came with the lucrative promotion of being in charge of all personnel decisions. But Newsome would have to move from Cleveland, where his career had spanned three decades.

Newsome's most controversial career decision was easy in many ways.

"It wasn't like I had another offer," Newsome told a team official.

The Ravens didn't have an identity in 1996, but with Newsome, the franchise had a vision. His philosophy has been to run the ball on offense and bully opponents on defense. More importantly, he seeks players who are emotional, hard-nosed, and bring a passion for the game. Every player who has put on a Ravens jersey, whether drafted by the Ravens or signed as a free agent, has to receive Newsome's approval.

Newsome has built two Super Bowl championship teams and has a reputation as being one of the NFL's top decision makers.

The Ravens won in 2000 with a record-setting defense that featured six starters from the franchise's first four drafts. Baltimore hoisted up the Lombardi Trophy in 2012, this time on the strength of its offense, which included seven starters drafted by Newsome.

His instincts have served him well over the years. After retiring as the NFL's most prolific pass-catching tight end in 1990, he passed on a position in the Browns' community relations department. He was a special assignment scout at first, before joining Bill Belichick's staff as an assistant coach.

The turning point for Newsome came in 1993, when Belichick released popular quarterback Bernie Kosar and offered the job of running the offense to Newsome. He declined and was named the director of pro personnel the next season for the Browns.

"I've never been around anyone before who has picked this up faster than Ozzie," said Ernie Accorsi, the former Cleveland Browns general manager.

The decision that has defined Newsome's tenure with the Ravens was also his first major one for the fledging franchise. Baltimore had the No. 4 overall pick and was in desperate need of star power to lure ticket holders and a big-name running back. Modell's preference was Lawrence Phillips, a troubled but talented runner from Nebraska.

Sitting at the top of Newsome's draft board was UCLA offensive tackle Jonathan Ogden. The Ravens, though, had a dependable left tackle in Tony Jones and didn't need an offensive lineman.

"Ozzie said, 'Jonathan Ogden will be a perennial Pro Bowl player, will play for this franchise for his career, and will have a decent shot at going into the Hall of Fame,'" Modell said. "What a Babe Ruth call that was."

Newsome got his way and used the Ravens' first draft pick on Ogden. Just as Newsome predicted, Ogden went to 11 Pro Bowls, played his entire 12-year career with the Ravens, and was inducted into the Hall of Fame in 2013.

Ogden asked Newsome to present him at his Hall of Fame induction. In the days leading up to the ceremony, Newsome reflected on the significance of the first player he ever drafted.

"If we don't pick Jonathan Ogden with that first pick," Newsome said, "I may not have this job."

The brilliance of Newsome is, when he makes mistakes, he learns from them. Before the 1997 draft, director of pro personnel James Harris suggested trading a second-round pick for a first-round choice in 1998 if given the opportunity. The San Diego Chargers eventually called the Ravens with that very offer, but Newsome declined because he wanted to take linebacker Jamie Sharper. That second-round pick would've turned into the No. 2 overall one in the 1998 draft.

Two years later, the Atlanta Falcons approached Newsome with the exact offer: the Ravens' second-round pick in 1999 for the Falcons' first-round choice in 2000. The opportunity wasn't met with open arms in the Ravens' draft room because Baltimore had already sent three draft picks to Detroit (for quarterback Scott Mitchell), St. Louis (for quarterback Tony Banks), and New England (for tight end Lovett Purnell).

When Newsome accepted the trade, coach Brian Billick and director of college scouting Phil Savage both walked out of the room in disgust. It's the only time Newsome went down to a press conference alone.

The Ravens used that pick, which turned into the No. 5 overall one in 2000, on what would be the offensive catalyst on the Ravens' Super Bowl team—running back Jamal Lewis.

"It was clear in my mind: make the trade," Newsome said. "It wasn't a popular thing in the room. But I have to keep the big picture in mind."

In 2002, Newsome was promoted to general manager, becoming the first African American to ever hold that position in the NFL. It paved the way for the Houston Texans' Rick Smith, the New York Giants' Jerry Reese, the Detroit Lions' Martin Mayhew, the Oakland Raiders' Reggie McKenzie, and the Arizona Cardinals' Rod Graves.

Newsome's results have been just as historic. In 17 drafts, Newsome has selected 17 players who have made a total of 53 Pro Bowl appearances. One of those players is already in the Hall of Fame (Ogden) and two are expected to eventually get there (Ray Lewis and Ed Reed).

On the Ravens' 2012 Super Bowl team, 38 of the 53 players were homegrown, meaning they were either drafted by Baltimore or signed with the team as undrafted free agents.

"There is no us without Ozzie," coach John Harbaugh said. "Ozzie is the foundation of the Ravens."

Jonathan Ogden

Jonathan Ogden was one of the most powerful offensive tackles to ever play the game. He was among the most agile blockers to ever protect a quarterback's blind side.

You can also make the case that Ogden was the smartest Ravens player.

He carried a 3.33 grade-point average as a history major at UCLA. When he went to run on the treadmill at Ravens headquarters, he always carried a book, usually the latest science fiction novel.

Ogden wasn't so much a student of the game. He was that kid in school who never studied but aced every test.

Consider this: Ogden's 11 Pro Bowl selections—he went every year after his rookie season—are a product of watching only a half-hour of film per week on his own.

The secret of Ogden's success was his notebook.

It was a personal journal of sorts in which he kept detailed notes on every defensive end he played twice, and it proved more beneficial to him than overloading on game film. With a few flips of a page, he could tell whether a player relied more on speed or power, a swim move or a clubbing style, quick feet or strong hands.

"They always say the quarterback and offensive linemen need to be the smartest—quarterback maybe, but O-line definitely," Ogden said. "It's all about how quickly you can read and process what's happening on the field and understand what the defense is trying to do to you. So definitely, the smarter you are, the less hesitation you have in what you're going to do, the better football player you're going to be. I always prided myself on never hesitating, because I always knew my assignment."

The beat-up spiral notebook suited Ogden's style. It wasn't flashy on the outside but contained a wealth of knowledge inside.

His well-grounded demeanor comes from his upbringing in Washington, D.C., where his father, Shirrel, was an investment banker, and his mother, Cassandra, was the executive director of a nonprofit organization that helped qualified minority students to get into law school.

Once one of the game's highest-paid players—he earned more than $30 million over his seven-plus-year career—Ogden never strayed far from his down-to-earth roots.

He drove his 1996 Range Rover (the one he bought after his senior year at UCLA) for years when he made his journey from Baltimore to his Las Vegas home, and he is more comfortable in T-shirts and jeans than in Armani suits. His teammates once said they only saw him wear one pair of shoes—open-toed leather sandals.

"That's just me," Ogden said. "I don't need to have five pairs of sandals. I like the ones I got. It has nothing to do with not wanting to spend money. I just like what I have."

There was a similar comfort zone when Ogden lined up on the left side.

When pulling to the outside on running plays, the 6-foot-9, 345-pound Ogden was like a runaway tractor-trailer coming at you full speed downhill. On passing plays, edge rushers were lucky if they saw the quarterback, much less got within reach of him.

Ogden once shut down Jacksonville Pro Bowl defensive end Tony Brackens so badly in the first half of a game that the Jaguars basically turned him into an outside linebacker in the second half, dropping him into coverage.

He once blocked Oakland Raiders defensive tackle Warren Sapp so hard on a running play that Sapp said afterward he thought Ogden had broken his ribs.

Hall of Fame defensive end Bruce Smith said of facing Ogden, "I know when I walk up to the line of scrimmage and I have to look up, I only think to myself, 'What in the world did his parents feed him?'"

Ravens defensive lineman Trevor Pryce remembered his only game against Ogden, playing him as a member of the Denver Broncos in 2005 just one season removed from having an injured back.

Said Pryce: "I tried to throw him off. ... In the middle of the play, he said: 'You can't do that. Your back's hurt. Are you all right?'"

Pryce then added, "In my 11 years of playing, he is by far the best I've ever played against."

Without Ogden, there wouldn't have been a Super Bowl championship in the 2000 season and there wouldn't have been a 2,000-yard rushing season for Jamal Lewis in 2003. Ogden was the Ravens' best offensive player and the one around whom the team built the offense.

It's fitting that the Ravens' first overall pick became their first homegrown player to reach the Hall of Fame. He put the franchise on the right path.

"When I came to Baltimore in 1996, we didn't even have team colors," Ogden said in his Hall of Fame speech in August 2013. "We just had a name. I can remember at the draft, I had that black jacket with the white letters that said 'Baltimore Ravens' and the white hat with the black letters that said Baltimore Ravens. And in the back of my mind, I was saying, 'I don't really know where we're going with this right now.' But Ozzie assured me: 'Our goal is to make a winner here.' I told him: 'I want to be a part of that.'"

Ogden's Hall of Fame career began on a humorous note. He took a red-eye flight from California to Baltimore in order to make rookie training camp. Ogden's mother called the Ravens to ask if he could skip the first day because he was tired.

"Yeah, so we sent him to his room with some milk and cookies," owner Art Modell said.

Ogden's impact extended beyond the Ravens. He redefined the tackle position. He was the ultimate protector of the Blind Side long before the movie made that term popular.

Teams have since been in search of their own Ogden, from Orlando Pace to Walter Jones to Joe Thomas. Still, there has never been an offensive tackle with his combination of speed, power, size, and athleticism. No one even came close.

The Ravens never had a franchise quarterback during Ogden's time. He blocked for 15 different starting quarterbacks. The Ravens never had a game-changing wide receiver, either. But they had Ogden, and he ruled the left side of the offensive line for 177 games—and he did so in a way that made it look effortless.

"He had no weakness," tight end Shannon Sharpe said. "He might have been the most complete offensive lineman to ever play the game."

Ogden was so respected that *USA Today* named him the No. 1 player in the NFL in 2003. He also stands tall among all the offensive linemen who have played the game.

"I've had the opportunity to be in this league for over 30 years, but in my opinion, there is not a player that played the position as well as Jonathan Ogden," Newsome once said.

Ogden's place in NFL history is now secured. In 2013, he became the first pure offensive tackle to get into the Hall of Fame in his first year of eligibility since Jackie Slater did it in 2001.

"You don't play to get in the Hall of Fame. You play to gain the respect of your peers," Ogden said. "Playing offensive line, you don't look for individual glory. But for the writers to say you're among the best players in the history of football, that's just breathtaking."

Ray Lewis

When Ray Lewis first stepped into the Ravens facility, he said he was going to be the best to ever play the game. Not best linebacker. Not best defensive player. The best player of all time.

Anyone would've rolled his eyes at Lewis, and for good reason. He was wearing dark sunglasses, a blue pinstriped suit, and gold chains around his neck. Lewis didn't look like the greatest player of all time. At 220 pounds, he didn't even look like a linebacker.

For the next 17 years, from 1996 to 2012, Lewis was determined to prove his point with every jarring tackle, crushing sack, timely interception, and game-winning play.

There was something special about Lewis, and it showed in his first NFL game, when he recorded a team-leading seven tackles and intercepted his first pass by picking off Billy Joe Hobert in the end zone. Lewis was named AFC Defensive Player of the Week, the first of many accolades that would come his way.

His credentials put him in a class by himself: 13 Pro Bowls, two Super Bowl victories, Super Bowl Most Valuable Player, and two-time NFL Defensive Player of the Year. He is just the sixth player in NFL history to win Defensive Player of the Year more than once, and the only inside linebacker to do it other than Mike Singletary.

What made Lewis legendary in this game was his ability to make others around him great. He had the uncanny ability to inspire teammates to raise their level of play. Lewis never quit, and he made sure you weren't going to either. Players said they couldn't make a mistake because they feared looking into Lewis' eyes after the play was over.

"From the very first time he walked through that door, people walked in behind him," said Bengals coach Marvin Lewis, who was the Ravens' defensive coordinator from 1996 to 2001. "When he walked into the huddle, the second practice that we had, he was already the leader of the team. He just had an innate sense of what it takes to be out front. He wasn't afraid to be out there."

Yet Ray Lewis made his biggest impression on coach Brian Billick during the 13th game of the 2000 season. After the Ravens defense had boasted all week about shutting out the lowly Browns, Cleveland took the opening drive 86 yards for a touchdown. As the players came off the field, Billick went to approach Lewis about what went wrong.

Lewis looked at Billick and said, "Don't say a thing, I got it." The Browns were held to 112 yards the rest of the game.

"I said, 'OK, anytime you want to do that, you go right ahead, Ray,'" Billick said. "I learned right then and there to stay out of the way."

Few got in Lewis' way on the football field in 2000, a year that began with him in handcuffs and ended with him on his way to hoisting up the Lombardi Trophy.

In January, he was charged with double murder in Atlanta. At 24, he faced an uncertain future and a tarnished reputation. Lewis eventually pleaded guilty to obstruction of justice and paid a $250,000 fine from the NFL.

"I live with that every day," Lewis said. "You maybe can take a break from it. I don't. I live with it every day in my life."

Credit: Mr. Schultz

The fans at opposing stadiums that year didn't let him forget it either. This journey made a tough team even tougher.

"I want to be very careful in characterizing how we benefited from this as a team because, at the end of the day, we've got to remind ourselves that there were two individuals that died that evening," Billick said. "To go through this with Ray, we knew in every city we went into, there were going to be certain attacks on Ray and the team. The challenge of that is something that I think brought this team together."

The Ravens didn't just rally around Lewis. They followed his lead, especially when it came to the playoffs.

In the AFC divisional playoff game at top-seeded Tennessee, Lewis delivered the decisive blow in the fourth quarter when he pulled a short pass away from running back Eddie George and ran it 50 yards for a touchdown.

"For me to make that play right there, I couldn't believe it myself," Lewis said. "Man-to-man coverage. I saw him bobble the ball. I snatched it out of his hand, [and] I saw the end zone. From there, it was history."

It soon became Super Bowl history. The Ravens went on to beat the Oakland Raiders in the AFC Championship Game and the New York Giants in the Super Bowl, where Lewis was named Most Valuable Player.

Lewis' statistics in the Super Bowl—five tackles and four passes defensed—weren't memorable. His impact was.

About nine minutes into the Super Bowl, Giants running back Tiki Barber got the ball on a sweep and had an alley if he could turn the corner. But Lewis read the play perfectly and chased down Barber from behind. It was, in Lewis' words, "a tone setter."

The Giants realized they had no chance running the ball against Lewis and were forced to put the ball in the hands of quarterback Kerry Collins, who threw four interceptions.

"Ray is responsible for that [trophy]," Modell said. "When he caught [Tiki] Barber from behind, that was the game. From that point on, we were in charge."

The football world saw Lewis' unmatched athleticism on display that game. What was often hidden was commitment to transforming his body into a machine and his tireless study of the game.

It was as much brain as brawn when it came to Lewis' success. He would watch film on Tuesday, the players' day off, and would know the other team's offense by the first practice Wednesday.

He often fell asleep at his computer while breaking down alignments and tendencies. Lewis loved winning the chess match with quarterbacks and often knew what was coming when teams lined up.

"You can hear him calling the plays out," quarterback Peyton Manning said. "He was going 'watch the screen, watch the screen!' I had to burn a timeout."

Lewis was both the most respected and feared defensive player of his generation. His passion for pain—to inflict it as well as absorb it—defined his unrelenting will.

He once hit Rashard Mendenhall so ferociously that he shattered the Pittsburgh running back's collarbone. On another occasion, he was so relentless that Cincinnati running back Corey Dillon refused to go back into the game in the fourth quarter.

There has never been a Raven as determined as Lewis. In 1997, his second season, Lewis ran down San Diego's Eric Metcalf after a 62-yard gain to the Ravens' 12-yard line. Metcalf had been clocked in the 40-yard dash at 4.3 seconds, and Lewis caught him and pulled him down with one hand.

Middle linebackers aren't supposed to do that, but Lewis showed time and time again that he wasn't your typical linebacker.

"I didn't think I would get there, because I didn't have a good angle," Lewis said. "I grabbed the back of his pads and snapped him down inside the 5."

That same resolve was on display in the 2002 season, when Lewis had the best start of his career. He recorded 45 tackles in his first three games and was putting on another dominant performance in Cleveland. But, midway through the third quarter, Lewis dove on a fumble by quarterback Tim Couch and he felt something pop in his left shoulder.

Lewis went over to the sideline, where his first thought was to do pushups. In his mind, if he could do them, he could play. So, he dropped to the ground and did about 15.

"I knew something was wrong, but I also know it's just one part of my body," Lewis said. "I got a whole part of me left that I'm willing to sacrifice for the men that are out there fighting with me. So my pain is put in the afterthought. I don't have time to think about that right now. And when I went back out there, I played, I think, like, eight, nine plays. And then, I got on the goal line, I ran into this guy—*pow!*—and I knew it was done."

Lewis added, "I don't call myself tough; I call me dealing with that injury tough, just because I made up my mind to say, 'No pain lasts always,'" Lewis said. "That's always my philosophy with pain: No pain lasts always."

With a mantra like that, it's no surprise that Lewis' favorite movie is "Gladiator" and that he fashioned himself as a warrior inside an arena every Sunday. The start of his gyrating pre-game dance, when Lewis picks up a tuft of grass and casts it into the wind, pays homage to the Russell Crowe flick. When the Ravens changed their home stadium to a synthetic field, team officials made sure there was a small piece of sod laying outside the tunnel. That's the power of No. 52.

Opposing players would line the sidelines to watch Lewis dance, and Lewis' phone was filled with numbers from those from around the league who reached out to him for advice. He was often called "the Godfather of the NFL."

There were other players who challenged him on and off the field. In 2003, an injured Joey Porter was so upset Lewis had mocked his celebratory "boot kick" move that he knocked on the side of the Ravens' team bus to instigate a fight. A handful of players had to hold back an irate Lewis.

Years later, a younger player on another team disrespected Lewis and called him "an old man" during a game.

"I looked at him and said, 'You'd better pray you play as long as me,'" Lewis said.

Lewis' storied career could've ended tragically. In 2012, he ripped his triceps muscle in Week 6 against the Dallas Cowboys. His season, and perhaps his 17-year run in the NFL, was presumed to be over.

But, at the age of 37, he unbelievably recovered in 10 weeks. "I told my team this would be my last ride," Lewis announced days before the Ravens' first playoff game in the 2012 season.

It was just in time for one last championship push and one last dance. In the wild-card win over the Indianapolis Colts, Lewis closed out his final home game in style, leading the Ravens with 13 tackles in what was a nostalgic and emotional farewell.

Moments before the final play of the game, coach John Harbaugh came up with the idea to line up Lewis at fullback as Joe Flacco took a knee. There were some anxious seconds as Lewis scrambled to find his helmet and get on the field before the ball was snapped.

"Remember you're on offense, so don't tackle the quarterback this time," an assistant coach jokingly said to Lewis.

As the final seconds ticked off the clock, Lewis did his dance near the middle of the field before getting swarmed by teammates. After a couple of interviews, Lewis noticed there were thousands of fans in the stands and made a lap around the stadium, holding his injured right arm high in the air.

Throughout the rest of the playoffs—from Denver to New England—fans came to games with billboards that read "Ray Lewis Retirement Party" on them. Lewis, though, was the one who continued to celebrate.

With his arm in a bulky brace, Lewis led the NFL in two categories—postseason tackles and determination.

"If I miss anything about my career, it's listening to what people say you can't do and then go do it," Lewis said.

Super Bowl XLVII, his final game, Lewis wasn't the MVP this time. He didn't have anything to do with the Ravens stopping the 49ers on fourth down at the Baltimore five-yard line. He didn't have a memorable tackle.

This time, after carrying this franchise for nearly two decades, it was his teammates' turn to give Lewis a gift that he will cherish for the rest of his life. He joined an elite group of players—John Elway,

Jerome Bettis, and Michael Strahan—to leave the game on top. His 12 years between Super Bowls is the longest span by any NFL player.

"When you're in our business, to have two rings on my right hand now is the ultimate," Lewis said. "There's no better way to go out. I can hold this the rest of my life and know I went out a champ."

Lewis will be eligible for the Pro Football Hall of Fame in 2018.

Matt Stover

The weight of scoring points for an entire month in the Ravens' first Super Bowl season fell on a 178-pound kicker.

"It was basically 52 other guys riding on his back," defensive end Rob Burnett said of Matt Stover. "And his leg held up."

Stover scored 49 straight points for the Ravens during a five-game stretch in which the offense failed to score a touchdown. He was called "Mr. October" by some teammates due to the fact that he was the only Ravens player to score during that entire month in 2000. And because of Stover, the Ravens amazingly won two of those games.

"I didn't realize I was scoring all of our points during that stretch until the fourth game," Stover said. "And it turns out that the games we won [12-0 over the Cleveland Browns at home and 15-10 over the Jacksonville Jaguars on the road] were the first back-to-back wins in the NFL where the kicker scored the only points since 1929."

It got to the point where Stover was the team's only sure thing in terms of scoring.

During one close game, coach Brian Billick and offensive coordinator Matt Cavanaugh were discussing what play to call on third down on the opponents' side of the field. That's when Stover heard several defensive players barking at the coaches.

"They were saying: 'Just kick it! Kick it! Don't even go for it, just fall on it, or kick it now!'" Stover said.

Stover will go down as one of the most accurate kickers in NFL history. When he retired in May 2011, his 2,004 career points were the fourth most in league history and his 83.7 percent career success rate was the seventh highest of all time.

No kicker was more successful outdoors during his career than Stover. He was actually more accurate when he was subjected to the elements than he was indoors.

His consistency on the field and commitment to the community off of it made him one of the most popular figures in team history. Fans wore his No. 3 jersey to games, something most NFL kickers would never see. A local rock station produced a musical tribute to Stover, changing the lyrics of Chris Daughtry's song "It's Not Over" to "It's Matt Stover."

"He's one of the better men that I've ever been around my whole life," linebacker Ray Lewis said. "He's a class guy. You know that in clutch times, Stover is always going to be there."

It's a chilling thought that Stover was nearly cut a year before the Ravens' championship season. In 1999, there was increasing friction between Billick and Stover.

Billick had just come from Minnesota, where kicker Gary Anderson didn't miss one field goal in the regular season. And, in Billick's first season in Baltimore, Stover was not performing as expected. Stover missed half of his first 10 field goal tries in 1999. He failed to convert two 54-yarders and had one blocked from 51 yards.

Billick put the pressure on Stover when he brought in kicker Joe Nedney, who was known for his strong leg. Stover thought there was a chance that his Ravens career was over.

The crux of the problem was Billick always asking Stover if he could make a kick in front of the entire team on the sideline.

"I went up to [Billick] and actually spoke to him man to man," Stover said. "I explained to him that if you ask me in front of the team if I can make it, I'm going to tell you yes every single time. Any man is going to say that in front of his boys. But if you can trust me and know that if I give you the 32-yard line as my limit, don't ask me for another yard. If that's not good enough, you have to cut me."

From that point forward, Stover told Billick his limit for that particular day after pre-game warm-ups. Stover then made everything he attempted, all 18 field goals for the remainder of that season, and Nedney was never activated.

Billick apologized to Stover later that season for handling him wrong.

"I was able to tell him thank you for trusting me and that I hope we have a long relationship," Stover said. "And we did."

Stover got the respect of his teammates in a more unusual way, thanks to the creative mind of defensive tackle Tony Siragusa.

"Goose gets in my ear at practice and tries to throw me off my game," Stover said. "One time when I was kicking, he pulled his pants down and gave me a big moon shine. If I can handle that, I can handle anything. And I nailed it."

"He said, 'OK, I give up.'"

In terms of Ravens history, Ray Lewis will go down as the Ravens' best defensive player, and Jonathan Ogden will be remembered as the best on the offensive side of the ball. When it comes to special teams, there was no one better than Stover.

Reliability characterized Stover's career. He kicked 19 game-winning field goals for the Ravens and was 24-for-24 in the fourth quarter from 2006 to 2008.

Stover's biggest game-winning kick just happened to be his final field goal for the Ravens. His 43-yard field goal with 53 seconds remaining lifted the Ravens to a 13-10 win at the Tennessee Titans and propelled Baltimore to the AFC Championship Game in January 2009.

"I thought, *if it's meant to be, that's the kick*. So I didn't screw up," Stover said. "It was a good way to leave. There was no regret."

Stover will be remembered for more than one kick. The lasting image of the only placekicker in the franchise's first 13 seasons is Stover raising his hands after every kick and pointing skyward.

It started in 1994 when Stover was with the Browns and had come into "a deep faith." One time, when Stover was playing for the Ravens, a referee approached him with a confused look on his face.

"Did I just see you point up after you missed that kick?," the referee asked.

After Stover replied yes, the referee said, "Amen, brother. That's the first time I've ever seen that. I always see it when the guys do something good but never bad."

Stover officially retired in May 2011 after playing one season for the Indianapolis Colts, and it was immediately announced that he was going into the Ring of Honor that season. As a measure of Stover's importance to the franchise, Ravens owner Steve Bisciotti sat next to Stover during the retirement announcement.

"I gave it all I had," Stover said. "I can look back at that and say I did all I could to be everything I could be."

David Modell

If David Modell had his way, America's Team would reside in Baltimore, not Dallas.

Modell's first choice for the name of the new Baltimore football team in 1996 was Americans, a nod to the Baltimore-Ohio train known as the American.

"I had this whole thing in my head of the charging locomotive look, steel gray, and most importantly with the American flag on the side," said Modell, who served as a Ravens executive from 1996 to 2003. "From Day One, you could argue, who is America's Team? And it's an explosion of interest in the team."

So, what happened to the name Americans? It never had a chance, much like Art Modell's thoughts of using the colors on the Maryland state flag (black and red) as his team's primary look.

In a *Baltimore Sun* poll that drew 33,288 responses, the Ravens got 66.4 percent of the calls. Modell's Americans finished a distant second with 16.8 percent.

"The voice of the fans was so strong and clear that it really didn't matter," Modell said.

Making a connection with the team's new fan base was essential to Modell. It's one of the reasons why he answered his own phone, something that's unheard of for NFL team presidents.

One of his first challenges was changing the fans' thinking when it came to a modern football facility. The new downtown football stadium would look different from Memorial Stadium, where the Ravens played their first two seasons.

Modell wanted to show fans how much higher the lower deck seats would stand in the new place and how much closer to the field they would be. The Ravens set up a stepladder at the exact height and location on the Memorial Stadium field with a sign in front of it that read: "This is where the first row of the lower deck will be in the new stadium." The team invited fans to climb up to sit there during games.

"It was very high tech," Modell said with a laugh. "We did bizarre things. We knew we needed to change some perceptions."

The other challenge was selling suites to a stadium that hadn't been built. The Ravens transformed an office space downtown with the same dimensions and furnishings as a luxury box.

"We had to paint the wall, in perspective, as if you were sitting in the suite looking out into the stadium. It's unbelievable what we got away with," Modell said. "Without going through some huge expense and spending all kinds of dough, we sold using a painted wall."

The effect was so convincing that someone from the fire department had wandered into the room and headed right toward the fake door on the wall before Modell stopped him.

"I'm thinking, *I hope we don't have a fire*," Modell said. "These guys aren't going to know how to get out of the building."

When it came to finding a new head coach, Modell had to be just as creative. After the Ravens fired their first coach, Ted Marchibroda, on December 28, 1998, the reported first choice was Mike Holmgren, the Super Bowl–winning coach who was resigning from the Packers.

The Modells had a private plane on the ground in Green Bay waiting to take Holmgren to Baltimore for the head-coaching job. Instead, Holmgren went to Seattle to meet with Seahawks owner Paul Allen, the co-founder of Microsoft and the 53rd-richest person in the world.

"Holmgren got on the much larger aircraft that was sent by Seattle," Modell said. "We had this little rubber band thing. So, off he went."

Modell had a second choice. In fact, he already had a first interview with this candidate before he fired Marchibroda, a decision that still bothers Modell.

When the Ravens played host to Minnesota on December 13, Modell greeted Vikings offensive coordinator Brian Billick after he stepped off the bus and asked to see him on the field. During pre-game warm-ups, Modell and Billick stood talking on the Ravens' shield at the 50-yard line for anyone to see.

"I didn't offer him a job. I didn't talk to him about a job. It wasn't like I was tampering with him per se," Modell said. "I just wanted to meet him. I wanted to see what his bearing was. I wanted to see what he was like. Nonetheless, it was obvious to us both what I was doing."

Just 37 days later, Billick was introduced as the second coach in Ravens history. And two years later, the Ravens were celebrating their first Super Bowl triumph.

Since the Ravens became the Ravens, Modell worked hard to make the fans feel like they were part of the team. It was now time for them to feel like they were part of a championship team.

After the Ravens won the 2000 Super Bowl, Modell stayed long after the game and let remaining Ravens fans pass the statue around the stands. It has since gone everywhere from Ravens' fan club meetings to a Super Bowl celebration for defensive tackle Tony Siragusa.

Modell estimates hundreds of thousands of fans have touched what he once called "the people's trophy."

Since Baltimore won the trophy, it's never been polished. Not once. That's the way Modell wants it.

"She has the fingerprints of everyone who has touched her," Modell said. "So when you touch the trophy, it's like you're touching all those who have touched it before you."

Chapter 2

THE TRANSITION PERIOD

Ted Marchibroda

Ted Marchibroda, the first coach of the Ravens, didn't deliver a championship. He couldn't bring a winning season in his three years with the team.

Marchibroda, though, did leave a legacy. He was the one who defined "Play Like A Raven" long before the franchise adopted it as its mantra.

Most coaches want the biggest and fastest players on their team. For Marchibroda, he eyed the ones who had a passion for the game and wanted to practice. This remains part of the Ravens' foundation for scouting players.

When the Ravens won their first Super Bowl in 2000, 21 players on the 53-man roster were brought onto the team during the Marchibroda era, which lasted from 1996 to 1999.

Why did the Ravens only win 16 games under Marchibroda? He was a good coach in a bad situation.

When Marchibroda first walked into the Ravens' facility, which had previously been used for police training, the drywall was still unfinished, boxes were still packed, and phone lines weren't connected. The team didn't even have official colors, and the season was set to begin in five months.

The players wore bland white and black uniforms at their first practice under Marchibroda. Owner Art Modell quipped, "We out Penn-Stated Penn State." The uniforms actually resembled the ones worn by the Mean Machine, the prisoners' team in the movie "The Longest Yard."

The Ravens weren't an expansion team. Those teams get two years to prepare. This was a challenge that no team since has had to undertake.

"We were all on the mountain," Ozzie Newsome said. "We didn't know how far we had to climb, but we just had to keep climbing. It was tough on Ted, tough on all of us."

When Modell decided to move the Ravens, he knew he couldn't bring along Bill Belichick as his coach. Critics point to this as another misstep by Modell because Belichick went on to win three Super Bowls for the New England Patriots.

But Modell needed someone to drum up publicity and sell tickets. The cantankerous Belichick didn't fit that role.

Modell was very aware that the past sells in Baltimore. After failing to steer Don Shula to the Ravens, Modell set his sights on Marchibroda, a former head coach of the Baltimore Colts.

Marchibroda was the anti-Belichick. He was a coach who brought a positive and gentle approach. He was one of pro football's nice guys.

Taking over the Ravens at the age of 65, Marchibroda had a grandfatherly approach. He walked through the Ravens locker room after preseason games and thanked each player individually for their efforts. He even once offered reporters potato chips after a win.

Longtime kicker Matt Stover described Marchibroda as a man of high character and integrity who was too old school for the changing NFL.

Training camps under Marchibroda started in early July and featured full-contact practices in the morning and night. Under Marchibroda, the Ravens often started fast, going 8-6 in September, but tired at the end of the season, losing seven of 11 games in December.

"I believe that he was past his time because he worked us crazy hard to where we had no gas left in the tank," Stover said.

There were other instances where Marchibroda showed he was past his prime. For instance, he would confuse Bennie Thompson with Ray Lewis, calling the special teams ace "Ray" when passing him on the stairs.

"I said, 'Poor fella, he don't know what he don't know,'" Thompson said.

Marchibroda did know how to put an electric offense on the field. Ask Marchibroda about his favorite book and he'd say: "the playbook."

The Ravens offense ranked in the top 10 in his first two seasons, and the Baltimore offense hasn't ranked higher than 13th since.

While the Ravens generated points, the wins were scarcer. Marchibroda had a history of turning teams around. He helped breathe life into the Colts in 1975, turning a 2-12 team in to a 10-4 division winner.

Marchibroda couldn't repeat that success with the financially challenged Ravens. During his first two seasons, Marchibroda was hand-cuffed by a team that had to pay for years of bad deals and had very little room under the salary cap. The Ravens had to cut players like linebacker Pepper Johnson, wide receiver Andre Rison, and cornerback Don Griffin just to sign their top two draft picks, Jonathan Ogden and Ray Lewis.

That also forced the Ravens to sign such forgettable free agents as Mike Croel, Jerrol Williams, and Keith Goganious, and go without a practice squad in 1996.

"The way our salary-cap situation was, we didn't have the ability to bring in a lot of the players he needed to win," Newsome said. "We had [undrafted rookie] Sedric Clark going against [five-time Pro Bowl offensive tackle] Tony Boselli in that first year. Heck, Ted [Marchibroda] and I do know a little football. We know we're not going to win in that matchup."

Times were so bad for the Ravens in these early years that team officials didn't know whether to laugh or cringe with embarrassment.

In 1997, five Ravens coaches and two Jaguars assistants got stuck in a Memorial Stadium elevator trying to get from the locker room to the coaches' box at halftime. The coaches missed nearly half of the third quarter.

Despite the challenges, the expected as well as the unexpected ones, one of Marchibroda's favorite sayings to his players was "Don't forget to fight."

The Ravens did fight to the end for Marchibroda, beating the Detroit Lions, 19-10, in his final game. It was also the last game for Hall of Fame running back Barry Sanders, and the Ravens held him to 41 yards rushing.

"It's been an uphill battle for three years and sometimes the battle defeats you," Marchibroda said after the game. "I can leave here and I can walk the streets of Baltimore with my head held up high."

A day after the season ended, Art Modell fired Marchibroda and cried while doing so.

Vinny Testaverde

The best quarterback in Ravens history before Joe Flacco came along was Vinny Testaverde.

He scored the franchise's first touchdown. He was among the team's first Pro Bowl players.

For a franchise whose identity later became a dominating defense, the best part of the Ravens' early days was Testaverde slinging the ball all over Memorial Stadium to Michael Jackson, Derrick Alexander, and Jermaine Lewis.

But the Ravens reached the end zone for the first time on, of all things, Testaverde's legs. Not known as a scrambler, Testaverde couldn't find an open receiver and raced nine yards for the touchdown before any Oakland Raider defender could touch him. Testaverde handed the ball to a fan.

"We didn't want to disappoint anyone," Testaverde said. "We could feel the enthusiasm pumping in from the stands. It was a great beginning for this franchise."

Testaverde was the starting quarterback for most of the team's first two years in Baltimore. He threw for 4,177 yards and 33 touchdowns in 1996, when he made his first Pro Bowl.

It looked like the Ravens had turned the corner in 1997, when Testaverde led them to a 3-1 start. But he failed to win eight of his next nine starts and never played for the Ravens again.

Some of the blame can be put on the Ravens' shoddy defense. Six of Testaverde's 20 losses in Baltimore came when the Ravens scored at least 25 points.

But Testaverde hurt himself more than any opposing defense ever did. Mixed in with his flashes of brilliance were costly fumbles and head-shaking decisions.

The biggest mistake Testaverde will be remembered for was slipping on The Meadowlands artificial turf, which was slick from a downpour, and, under no pressure, threw the ball while on his knees. It was picked off to kill a critical third-quarter drive.

"As soon as it left my hands, I thought of Brett Favre and the one he threw like that earlier in the season," Testaverde said. "Big mistake."

That one-crucial-mistake label always has been stitched to Testaverde. It started when he threw the last of his five interceptions, near the end zone in the final seconds of the 1987 Fiesta Bowl, and his favored Miami team lost to Penn State for the national championship. It continued throughout his 21-year NFL career.

Bouts of inconsistency were his downfall, and it didn't help that he was an introvert at the most important take-charge position in the game. Testaverde lacked the tough-guy leadership, and his teammates lost faith in his ability to win close games.

In December 1997, punter Greg Montgomery decorated a 3-foot Christmas tree in the locker room. It was telling that it featured a Testaverde figurine hanging by its neck.

Seven months later, the Ravens officially released Testaverde, even though he had cleared out his locker long before and the Ravens had gone through workouts with Jim Harbaugh as their starting quarterback.

"Even when I was in Tampa Bay, they never showed me this type of disrespect," Testaverde said at the time. "I've been in the league 11 years—five years with the same organization. I think I deserve better."

Testaverde added, "First they couldn't get Jim Kelly, for whatever reasons, then they went out and got Jim Harbaugh. Maybe I should change my name to Jim."

The divorce was a bitter one, but Testaverde's name remains a fixture in the Ravens' record books. He was the franchise's all-time passer for 11 years after his departure until Kyle Boller surpassed him. And Testaverde still holds the mark for the most passing yards against the Ravens when he threw for 481 yards against their record-setting defense as the quarterback for the New York Jets in 2000.

Bennie Thompson

To excel at special teams, you have to be crazy. And there was no one crazier than Bennie Thompson.

The Ravens' proud history of special teams aces began with Thompson, who played with relentlessness, passion, and sometimes without some vital equipment.

In 1997, Thompson had his helmet knocked off at midfield and still ran 20 more yards through a wedge to make a tackle against the Steelers. An energized Thompson ran to the end zone to celebrate with the crowd before heading back to the sideline where, to his surprise, a teammate handed his helmet back to him.

"I didn't even know my helmet was off," Thompson said. "All I knew was I had to make the tackle. If I didn't, they were going to split the middle and go all the way with it."

Thompson recorded nearly 200 special teams tackles during his 11-year career and earned a trip to the Pro Bowl as a member of the Ravens in 1998.

He will be remembered as the best special teams tackler in Ravens history. It's not because of numbers. It's because of his commitment to the game.

Team doctors never told Thompson how much time he would miss before a surgery because they knew he would refuse the operation. In each of his four seasons with the Ravens, Thompson broke his left hand and had to play with a cast. It became one of the Ravens' earliest traditions.

Trying to keep Thompson from playing was almost as impossible as blocking him. One night before the Ravens were to play the Steelers, one of the four pins in his dislocated wrist came out. He played the next day.

"Players looked at my pins coming through my skin and said, 'Eww, are you playing?' I'm like, 'Yeah, I'm playing. This ain't going to keep me out of a game,'" Thompson said. "The doctor put some oil or something on it, wrapped my hand up real tight, and I went out and played."

When Thompson played, the Ravens knew they were going to get his best. They just didn't know what else they were getting.

In a game against Jacksonville, Thompson walked through the Jaguars huddle three times pointing at players.

"You know how Michael Jordan gets into that zone where no one can stop him," Thompson said. "I get into a talking zone, man. I can't shut up. There is only one Bennie in this world."

There was a time he covered a punt against the Bengals and watched it bounce seven times before he scooped it up, threw it at a player, and acted like he recovered a fumble.

"The officials had made so many bad calls that year, you might be able to get away with anything," Thompson said.

Thompson had fun while playing, but few played with more intensity. He was always the first player to arrive at the Ravens facility at 7 a.m. He ran on the StairMaster for an hour and lifted weights before attending meetings and practicing.

A day after coach Ted Marchibroda complained about players not having the proper attitude during practice, Thompson exchanged punches with Earnest Hunter and threw the running back's helmet 30 yards.

"To me, if we had 52 guys like Bennie Thompson, we'd be in the Super Bowl every year," strength coach Jerry Simmons said.

When the Ravens did make their first Super Bowl, Thompson was an assistant coach and not a player.

The Ravens asked Thompson to retire before the 2000 season began, after 11 seasons as one of the best special teamers in the league. He obliged.

"Bennie Thompson can still play, make no mistake about that," coach Brian Billick said at the time. "He's a little bit of a victim of the system in what you have to pay a vested veteran. We all know Bennie would play for less if they'd let him."

Thompson can recall standing next to former New York Giants coach Bill Parcells during the National Anthem of the Super Bowl.

Parcells asked him: "What would you give to play in this game right now?"

Thompson responded, "I would give up my life."

Thompson sacrificed so much during his time with the Ravens that it shouldn't matter how he earned a ring. When Thompson wears it, many fans think he got it as a player.

"I don't tell them any different," Thompson said.

Michael Jackson

The Ravens lacked many things in their early years, but thanks to wide receiver Michael Jackson, there was no shortage of flash.

One of the Browns who relocated to Baltimore, Jackson arrived wearing one gold earring and driving a Mercedes convertible. It sat outside the club at every party he hosted in Baltimore.

Jackson's closet was equally legendary.

"All of us on the team had one or two suits," offensive lineman Wally Williams said. "Michael had a collection."

Jackson's wardrobe consisted of 30 custom-made suits, each with matching alligator shoes.

"Michael is a tall, lanky guy. He looked even taller in the suits," Williams said. "His jacket alone was six feet tall."

Along with quarterback Vinny Testaverde, Jackson was one of the early faces of the franchise when it moved to Baltimore. He was one of the three players invited to the city when the team's name was unveiled and one of the first to model the new uniforms at a downtown event.

Always one to stand out in a crowd with that warm smile and bald head, Jackson had radio and TV deals in town. He was also one of the first and last to sign autographs for fans during training camp.

The unexpected move of the team coincided with a surprising transformation with Jackson on the field. After playing in the shadow of Andre Rison in Cleveland, Jackson became a go-to receiver for the first time in his six-year NFL career.

Jackson used his long arms, especially on stiff-arm maneuvers, and leaping ability to overmatch shorter cornerbacks. At 6 feet 4, he simply out-jumped defenders for many of his NFL-best 14 touchdowns in 1996.

It was more than a physical game for Jackson. He liked to bait defenders before the snap, telling them what route he was going to run.

"Some [cornerbacks] would take heed, but most didn't," Jackson told *The Baltimore Sun.* "In those situations, the truth is the last thing a person will believe."

In his 10th game as a Raven, he confronted a fan in Jacksonville who was heckling him from his seat in the end zone.

"I told the guy, 'I'm going to catch a touchdown pass right here, in this [left] corner, and then I'll throw the ball to you,'" Jackson said.

Backing up his words, he caught a five-yard touchdown pass from Vinny Testaverde just before halftime in that left corner of the end zone. Jackson then launched the ball toward the stands.

"I must have thrown it pretty hard, because the [NFL] fined me $500," he said.

He was almost a man of his word earlier that season. In the Ravens' first-ever preseason game, Jackson promised fans at Memorial Stadium a touchdown.

"I went down to the far corner and I talked with people, signed a few autographs," Jackson said. "I told them that I was going to score it on that end, but I scored it on the other end."

Jackson caught a 31-yard touchdown pass from Testaverde in the preseason win over the Philadelphia Eagles. The points scored by that catch were the first by a Baltimore player since the Colts moved to Indianapolis after the 1983 season.

Slowed by injuries, Jackson became a free agent in 1998 and decided to retire at the age of 30. He eventually moved back to his hometown of Tangipahoa, Louisiana, and served as mayor until 2012.

Bam Morris

Byron "Bam" Morris represented another reclamation project for Ravens owner Art Modell.

After the Ravens passed on troubled running back Lawrence Phillips in the 1996 draft, the team addressed that position of need by picking up Morris following his release from the Pittsburgh Steelers.

Morris came to the Ravens after pleading guilty to a drug charge and wasn't re-signed two years later while serving jail time over a probation violation.

In between his legal troubles, Morris provided one of the first landmark wins for the franchise and gave the Ravens local bragging rights for years.

Morris rushed for a career-high 176 yards on a cold and wet day in Landover, Maryland, as the Ravens won, 20-17, and handed the Washington Redskins their first loss at Jack Kent Cooke Stadium. A large contingent of Ravens fans could be heard chanting "Bam" as they got a glimpse of a power running game that would become a staple of the offense in their playoff years.

"When he showed up to play, he showed up to play," offensive lineman Wally Williams said. "That was never a problem. Everybody has sort of a split personality that you have to deal with whether you're on the field or off the field. Maybe Bam had three personalities that he had to deal with."

There was Byron Morris, the upstanding character who cracked up teammates in the locker room.

There was Bam Morris, the bruising running back who led the Ravens in rushing in their first two years of existence.

And there was "Bamarama," the loose cannon who couldn't stay out of trouble when he walked out of the football facility.

Morris' off-the-field problems, including arrests for possession and trafficking of marijuana, eventually led to multiple convictions and prison time.

The Ravens announced in 1997 that they wouldn't re-sign Morris while he was serving a four-month jail term for violating probation in connection with his 1996 arrest for marijuana possession.

"I wish him the very, very best," Modell said at the time. "He's basically a good young man who needs direction, needs discipline, and needs to assume responsibility."

He was the embodiment of a pro athlete who blew his fortune on drugs, alcohol, and parties.

In July 2004, Morris was released from state prison after being locked up for almost five years. He went on to lead the National Indoor Football League's Katy Copperheads in rushing while earning $300 per game, a far cry from his $1.2 million salary at the height of his NFL career.

"I had everything, and then I lost it," Morris said. "Part of what I want to tell people is that I never looked at football as a job. I looked at it as a way to make money so I could party."

Nearly 20 years removed from his last game with the Ravens, Morris still ranks as the sixth-leading rusher in team history.

Wally Williams

Wally Williams made history when he became the first Ravens player to receive the franchise tag, a mechanism that kept the offensive lineman off the free agent market.

He just couldn't believe it when this happened in 1998.

"When it got to me that this was even a conversation, I was like: Man, are these people crazy?" Williams said. "I just never saw myself in that light. It happened and I'm [grateful for] that. I'm glad I made my mark in history. I'm happy that, at one point, the Ravens saw me in that light. I still wear that as a badge of honor today."

Even though Williams received $3 million that season, which was more than what the undrafted player had ever earned before, he sat out of training camp like many franchise-tag players have done over the years.

By the end of that season, coach Ted Marchibroda was preparing to get fired and wasn't blaming owner Art Modell. He pointed the finger at the offensive line, and more specifically, the absence of Williams over the summer. That year, the offensive line never developed as expected and the Ravens finished 20th in the NFL in rushing.

"If I didn't know [what went wrong], or if I wasn't 100 percent right, it would bother me," Marchibroda said. "And I'm not looking through rose-colored glasses for myself. We thought we'd be able to run the football. That's why we brought Jim [Harbaugh] in and Vinny [Testaverde] was let go."

Williams remains proud of his three years in Baltimore. He believes the offensive line that included Jonathan Ogden, Orlando Brown, and Jeff Blackshear played with a physical mindset that not only set the standard for the Ravens but also factored into the development of the franchise's best player.

Middle linebacker Ray Lewis learned some "harsh lessons" from practicing against this offensive line, which played an integral role in him developing into one of the top defensive players of his generation.

"It was a violent group of guys," Williams said. "We enjoyed the violence of the game and we took pride in that. We didn't mind sending you out of the game limping."

After starting 13 games in 1998—seven at left guard and six at center—Williams left Baltimore and signed a five-year, $18.5 million contract with New Orleans, where he was assured he wouldn't have to bounce around on the offensive line. This made Williams the only player to receive the franchise tag from the Ravens and not sign a lucrative, long-term deal with the team.

Williams, who is currently on sports talk radio in Baltimore, considers the Ravens his NFL home. He remembers being among the first people to lay a brick in the early stages of constructing the team's new downtown stadium.

"I look back and I'm proud of what I helped build in Baltimore," Williams said. "And, each year that goes by, I appreciate it even more."

Orlando Brown

Orlando Brown, the most bruising offensive lineman in Ravens history, struck fear in defensive linemen, his own teammates, and even mascots.

The 6-foot-7, 360-pound Brown chest-bumped so violently that everyone avoided him before games. The Ravens' mascot, Poe, learned the hard way before a game against San Francisco in 2003, when he got bowled over by Brown during player introductions.

"Our pre-games are dangerous, because he's hitting people and he doesn't care who it is," offensive coordinator Matt Cavanaugh said.

Brown was affectionately known as "Zeus," which came from his mother. She thought of it while she was pregnant with him and taught mythology at a junior high school. The nickname proved ironic because Brown weighed barely over three pounds when he was born a month premature. By the time he reached high school, he was 250 pounds.

Brown was a self-made man and a self-made player who never forgot his roots of growing up on the tough streets of Washington, D.C. His blocking style was more of a street brawler and his feet were far from being the quickest. Brown's success was due in large part to his uncommon size and relentless desire. Teammates believed Brown could break your sternum with a punch.

"You always tried to outsmart him because you couldn't beat him physically," defensive end Rob Burnett said. "If he got his hands on you on a passing play or got his body on you on a run, you might as well go back to the huddle."

Because he had to work so hard to earn a big contract in the NFL, Brown liked to beat up on first-round draft picks, even those on his own teams. That meant a tough initiation for Peter Boulware, who was the Ravens' top pick in 1997. Brown destroyed Boulware in his first two training camps.

"He's one of the strongest guys you'll ever play against," Boulware said. "His technique is straight intimidation. He's going to block you to the ground every time and try to punish you. That's just the way it is. There's no mercy, no grace with him."

Players say Brown wasn't a trash-talker. He was a noise-maker.

"Trash-talkers is talking about your momma and your kids and saying things like 'I'm going to get you.' He wasn't that type of guy," offensive lineman Wally Williams said. "But you knew he was over there and, nine times out of 10, you knew the guy lining up in front of him was having a problem. Because you first heard the grunts and then you heard the thuds."

Brown left the Ravens after the 1998 season and went back to play for Cleveland, where he made national headlines. On December 19, 1999, Brown was accidentally struck in the eye when referee Jeff Triplette threw a weighted penalty flag that somehow sailed through the bars of his face mask.

Brown was legally blind in the eye for months. It seemed doubtful he'd play again. Yet without as much as laser surgery, the eye slowly healed naturally.

"When I couldn't see out of [the eye], I was scared. I was like, 'Damn. What a way to go out,'" Brown said. "I always thought a player would hurt me."

Four years later, Brown was back in football and back with the Ravens. He was the Ravens' right tackle on an offensive line that paved the way for Jamal Lewis' 2,000-yard rushing season.

"He was like a big brother to me," Jamal Lewis said. "When they brought him over I was like, 'Wow! This guy is huge.' In games, a guy like Zeus would come to me and say, 'Just follow me, big boy.' As a running back, that's what you want to hear."

Emotions drove Brown on the field, and they sometimes were his downfall.

During halftime in a game at Miami, offensive line coach Jim Colletto was trying to make a point about blocking schemes, which set off Brown. He became so infuriated that he began tearing apart his locker, repeatedly yelling, "Just let me play the game!"

Colletto had to call coach Brian Billick to get involved. "Look at me," Billick told Brown. "If you can't look at me and you can't calm down, you can't play. He's only trying to make you better. You should know that."

Brown failed to keep his temper in check in the 20-17 playoff loss to the Tennessee Titans in 2003. The Titans thought they could sucker Brown into a rage, and they were right. He committed two personal-foul penalties, the latter of which may have cost his team the game.

"I screwed up, man," he said afterward.

Brown stopped playing in 2005 and was found dead six years later due to complications from diabetes. The medical examiner said there was no evidence Brown knew he had the disease.

Priest Holmes

The Ravens' great run of finding undrafted rookies—Bart Scott, Jameel McClain, Dannell Ellerbe, and Justin Tucker—began with running back Priest Holmes in 1997.

Holmes' knee injury and his status as Ricky Williams' backup at Texas kept him from being drafted. Even a 120-yard, three-touchdown rushing game in the Big 12 championship, after Williams was hurt, couldn't elevate him in the eyes of NFL teams.

The Ravens paid $2,500 to sign Holmes, who would eventually become the first undrafted rookie to win the NFL rushing title.

"A guy who's drafted late or is a free agent has to play his way into the league," said Phil Savage, who was the Ravens' director of college scouting from 1996 to 2002. "A guy who goes in the first four rounds has to play his way out of the league. Priest, from Day One, began playing his way into the league."

Despite Holmes' hard work, nothing came easy for him during his time with the Ravens. In his first three seasons, he played behind Bam Morris, Earnest Byner, and Jay Graham in Baltimore, yet he held club records for single-season rushing (1,008) and career rushing (1,514) in 1999.

His best games seemed to always come against the lowly Cincinnati Bengals, but his shining moment occurred in the 1998 season finale. It was a day when Holmes missed a chance to talk to Barry Sanders before the game and then outplayed the future Hall of Fame running back in his final game.

Holmes ran for 132 yards, which was 91 more yards than Sanders, in a 19-10 win over the Detroit Lions. And Holmes did this after bruising his thigh in an accidental collision with a teammate before the game.

"I would never say I outplayed [Sanders]," Holmes said after the game. "I look at him and I see how much work I still have to do."

Holmes never fit into what the Ravens had envisioned in their running game. He was a slashing runner, not a powerful one. There were some decision-makers who thought Holmes wasn't big enough to hold up for an entire season.

"We felt in order for us to grow as an offense, if we could get someone who could be a tackle-breaker, that would be beneficial to us," general manager Ozzie Newsome said.

It became clear that Holmes wasn't in the Ravens' future plans when they used the No. 5 overall pick on Jamal Lewis in 2000. Holmes, who held nine team rushing marks at the time, was relegated to being the third-down back.

"When you're on a winning team, there are certain players that have to fulfill certain roles, and I believe my role is definitely important to the team," Holmes said.

Known for being unselfish, Holmes went out of his way to show Lewis how to prepare for life in the NFL. Even after Lewis was drafted to take his job, Holmes still broke down game film with the rookie every Thursday night during the Super Bowl season, picking apart defenses and analyzing what running lanes to hit. Those words followed Lewis throughout his career.

"I call him my mentor," Lewis said. "We had that kind of bond."

Holmes became a free agent after the Ravens won the Super Bowl and he signed a modest contract with the Kansas City Chiefs, where he became one of the NFL's top offensive players for a four-year period. While he never produced the same type of numbers in Baltimore, his influence on Lewis helped the Ravens years after he was gone.

Chapter 3

A DOMINANT DEFENSE EMERGES

Marvin Lewis

Marvin Lewis was close to not being the mind behind the best defense in the NFL.

After Brian Billick was hired as the Ravens' new coach in 1999, Lewis had to interview for the defensive coordinator position, a job he had held with the Ravens for the previous three seasons.

Billick's first choice for defensive coordinator was Gunther Cunningham, and it didn't change after sitting down with Lewis for the first time.

"It was the most miserable interview in the history of interviews," Billick said. "He was emotionally down. By the time he left that interview, I'm thinking I not only don't want to make this guy my coordinator, I not only don't want him on my staff, I don't want to see the son of a bitch again."

It was a gut-wrenching time for Lewis. Billick could only promise a spot as a position coach to Lewis while assembling his staff, which meant Lewis had to line up other jobs even though he desperately wanted to stay in Baltimore.

What Lewis had going for him was he had earned the respect of Billick just a month earlier, when Lewis' defense played as well as anyone against Billick's high-scoring Minnesota Vikings offense.

Billick eventually realized Lewis was going through a tough time, and he decided to talk to him again. This time, they clicked.

"It was obviously better," Billick said. "I was immediately impressed."

Cunningham was promoted to become the Kansas City Chiefs head coach, and Billick hired Lewis.

The rest is NFL history, at least on defense.

Under Lewis, the 2000 Ravens allowed the fewest points ever (165) over a 16-game schedule. They allowed the fewest rushing yards (60.6 a game) over a 16-game schedule, too. Their four shut-outs were the most in the league since the 1976 Steel Curtain defense in Pittsburgh.

Lewis proved a team could win with unyielding defense in an age of overpowering offense.

Big-play linebackers, shut-down cornerbacks, and zone blitzes became his calling cards. Controlling the line of scrimmage, winning third-down battles, and forcing turnovers were the typical results.

The crowning moment for the defense came in the Super Bowl, when Lewis approached the Ravens' offensive players with one request prior to kickoff.

"Give us 10 points, and we'll win," Lewis said.

Lewis was right. The Ravens routed the New York Giants, 34-7, in capturing the Lombardi Trophy.

The Ravens gave up one offensive touchdown in the playoffs. The only points allowed by Baltimore in the Super Bowl came on a kickoff return. It marked only the third time in Super Bowl history that a defense held the opposing offense scoreless, with the other two coming in the 1970s:

The 1972 No-Name Defense from Miami.

The 1974 Steel Curtain Defense from Pittsburgh.

And the 2000 Ravens.

It was a throwback defense. It was a punishing one. The players followed Lewis' three commandments: "We run. We tackle. We stay on our feet."

What did Lewis do? He lit the fire by finding every piece of criticism and throwing it in their faces.

There were questions about Tony Siragusa's weight, Peter Boulware's ability to stay standing against blockers, Duane Starks' diminutive size, Rod Woodson's age, and Kim Herring's soft image.

"A lot of the guys were castoffs and they were very smart overachievers," Lewis said. "Collectively together, they were great. But they were castoffs. That was kind of their battle cry. They were players that not a lot of people wanted and they took that to heart."

The arrival of the Ravens' indomitable defense in Super Bowl XXXV is no overnight success story. This was five years in the making, a project launched in 1996 with the hiring of Lewis as defensive coordinator.

But, like his initial meeting with Billick, Lewis made a bad first impression with his players. When Lewis came to Baltimore in February 1996, fresh off a trip to the Super Bowl as the Pittsburgh Steelers' linebackers coach, he basically trashed the system the Ravens used when they were in Cleveland and reminded his new players how the Steelers did things in Pittsburgh.

That would've been fine if Lewis was coaching in the NFC. It's downright blasphemy when you're coaching a division rival. His first season as defensive coordinator was a disaster, as the Ravens gave up an average of 27.6 points per game, the third-most in the league.

Lewis molded the defense into his vision. By the time the Ravens were setting NFL records in 2000, Lewis had coached six starters since their rookie seasons and had a long history with another (Woodson).

The biggest lesson he taught them was to be unselfish. The Ravens became so truly dedicated to the scheme that defensive end Michael McCrary remained on the outside to contain instead of trying to work underneath for sacks. Starks quit jumping every route. And Woodson stopped shifting toward the middle of the field and stayed where he belonged.

"Most of the time, he put you in a position to make plays," defensive end Rob Burnett said. "There were no pawns out there. There were no guys out there just to take up space. Everyone had an opportunity to make plays in this defense, and it's fun to play."

Lewis is smart. Not just football smart. He routinely earned straight A's without bringing home books and was expected to be an engineer like his sisters after scoring over 1,200 on his SATs.

Instead, he used his brain to play football at Idaho State. Despite being undersized, he became an all-conference linebacker.

"I cheated all the time," Lewis said. "I wasn't very good. I just knew what the offense was going to do."

The "cheater" then became a coach.

During games, Billick would occasionally switch his headset to listen to Lewis' observations.

"It's amazing how many times they will come out in a certain formation and Marvin will be saying, 'Here comes the trap' or 'Here comes the boot.' And sure enough, that's what it was," Billick said. "He has an excellent eye for tendencies on what a team does. And what you continually try to do is make the players see it the same way."

Lewis left the Ravens after the 2001 season to become the defensive coordinator for the Washington Redskins. A year after that, he was hired to be the head coach of the Cincinnati Bengals in 2003 and just finished his 11th season there.

Rod Woodson

The first big free agent signing by the Ravens didn't make sense at first.

Why would Rod Woodson, a future Hall of Fame defender in the twilight of his career, want to sign with the Ravens in 1998? It was a franchise that had won only 10 games in its first two seasons.

And why would the Ravens want a 32-year-old cornerback with a bad knee? This was a franchise that had been focused on building with young players.

If the Ravens hadn't taken the chance on Woodson—and persuaded him to come to Baltimore—the team and linebacker Ray Lewis wouldn't be the same.

Woodson wasn't one of the top five defensive players on the field anymore, but his wisdom was an invaluable asset and his presence brought validity to a fledging franchise.

He knew how first-class organizations were run, having played for the Pittsburgh Steelers and San Francisco 49ers. He already had a place in NFL history after being named to the NFL's 48-man 75th anniversary team in 1994.

"Confidence in this league is that deciding factor in winning and losing, I believe," Woodson said. "My first year [in Baltimore], nobody had it. I wasn't used to going on the sideline and seeing guys saying, 'Oh well there it goes again.' I wasn't used to that. It was a fight. But I knew there was going to be a growing stage because the guys were so young."

It was a growing stage for Woodson as well. His declining speed and the Ravens' draft (they selected cornerbacks Duane Starks and Chris McAlister in the first round in 1998 and 1999) prompted the Ravens to move Woodson from cornerback to safety. But his role on the team never changed.

He was the on-field general who put players in the right position because he could anticipate what play was going to be run. It was never more evident than in one of the last regular-season games in the 2000 championship season.

On fourth down and five at the Baltimore 12-yard line, Woodson urged defensive coordinator Marvin Lewis to blitz the Arizona Cardinals. The Ravens put Ray Lewis up to the task, and he batted down Jake Plummer's pass to preserve the 13-7 victory.

Being the elder statesman on that defense was both fabulous and fleeting.

"In that one given year, we were arguably the best defense in NFL history," Woodson said. "The downside is that we were only together for one season."

On a team known for its trash-talking, Woodson was the voice of reason. He was also there to set an example for the Ravens' young defensive backs.

Woodson was not only brought in to show the Ravens how to win. He also showed them how to prepare to win.

"They see Rod come in here after being in the league for 10 or 11 years and he's taking notes and asking questions," Marvin Lewis said. "Whenever you take a break, he has another question: 'You said you wanted to play this that way. How about this way? What if they motion and do this? How about if he aligns there?' That makes those guys take notice."

The Ravens also put Woodson's locker next to that of Ray Lewis, who was in his third year at the time and already a Pro Bowl player.

He invited Lewis to join the team's defensive backs for happy hour every Friday at a local restaurant. Lewis would invite Woodson, whose family lived in Pittsburgh, to his house for home-cooked meals made by his mother.

"I was just being a friend, not judging him," Woodson said. "Anything he wanted to talk about, we talked about. That's what friends are. I mean, true friends don't judge anyone."

Woodson's influence put Lewis' rudderless life back on track, although he would never take credit for doing so.

Instead of seeking the spotlight, Woodson often deferred to Lewis. "Because Rod saw it was good for the team," coach Brian Billick said. "That says a lot about Rod Woodson. Sometimes guys demand that role, but he saw a purpose in Ray Lewis having it."

But Billick knows how valuable Woodson became to that defense.

"Our defensive strength grew in proportion to Rod's becoming more comfortable at the position," Billick said. "Rod was kind of an anchor for us. Obviously, by the time he came here, he had established Hall of Fame credentials."

Billick added, "At that point in his career, it was all about one thing—he had the big contracts, the Pro Bowls, the fame, and everything that goes with a Hall of Famer. But he did not have a ring. His purity of intentions was a great benchmark for us."

In 2000, Woodson's 14th season in the NFL, he captured that elusive Super Bowl ring. In 2009, he became the first player to ever wear a Ravens uniform to reach the Pro Football Hall of Fame.

Michael McCrary

No one wanted to win a Super Bowl more than defensive end Michael McCrary.

It could've been measured by his drive and passion. It also could be measured by his pain tolerance.

During the Super Bowl, McCrary broke his right hand when he smashed it against the helmet of safety Rod Woodson while trying to strip the ball away from New York Giants running back Tiki Barber. After going to the locker room for X-rays, he returned to collect his second sack of the game in the fourth quarter.

While teammates still celebrated the day after the game, a doctor performed a bone graft and inserted a plate, two pins, four screws, and a tension wire in McCrary's hand.

"Passion and accountability. We want players with those things," said Brian Billick, McCrary's head coach for four years. "No Raven better served those two characteristics than Michael. For him to sacrifice the way he did for us to win a Super Bowl, that was extraordinary."

A seventh-round pick by the Seattle Seahawks in 1993, McCrary was an undersized pass rusher who made a living by outworking his opponents.

Many of McCrary's 71 career sacks came from being the quickest defensive end on the field. But he got to the quarterback with hustle, racking up sacks by running down quarterbacks when they rolled to the other side. There were times when McCrary brought down the quarterback by crawling yards to get to him.

"I can honestly say I never took a play off," McCrary said. "I never wanted to be disappointed in the way I played. Even when we lost, I knew I had done my best every time."

McCrary was so distraught for messing up in the divisional playoff game in Tennessee that he was scribbling his assignments on his pants leg.

"Tears were running down his face," defensive coordinator Marvin Lewis said. "That's how serious he took it."

Ravens general manager Ozzie Newsome once said signing McCrary as a free agent in 1997 was the beginning of the record-setting defense that helped the Ravens win the 2000 Super Bowl. Even though the Ravens had drafted middle linebacker Ray Lewis a year earlier, the addition of McCrary allowed the Ravens to go from a 3-4 defense to a 4-3 one.

McCrary, though, wasn't the Ravens' first choice. The Ravens initially pursued Cardinals free agent Michael Bankston. When Bankston wanted too much money, Newsome set his sights on McCrary, who was waiting for a team to make a decent offer. McCrary had gone on free-agent trips to the Houston Oilers, Indianapolis Colts, and Philadelphia Eagles but never left with a contract.

McCrary's deal with the Ravens went on to define Newsome's mantra of "right player, right price." McCrary made two Pro Bowls for Baltimore and finished his career second on the Ravens' all-time sacks list with 51. Bankston, on the other hand, had 12.5 sacks in his final four seasons.

"He was the model for every player we went after," Newsome said of McCrary.

Teammates were as much in awe of McCrary's high motor as his off-the-wall personality. McCrary told so many crazy stories that defensive tackle Tony Siragusa nicknamed him, "Boy in the Bubble."

Some of McCrary's tales include seeing four-foot-tall jackrabbits around his offseason home in Arizona, owning a go-cart that can accelerate to 200 miles per hour, and using binoculars that can detect facial hair from 10 miles away.

Honestly.

"You look and you go on," defensive tackle Sam Adams said. "It's not embarrassing or bad for him because he believes all his stories. Who knows? I don't want to say you've never seen a 300-pound dog before. But come on, I've never seen a 300-pound dog and no one has ever seen that. You want to try to give him the benefit of the doubt until he goes too far."

Still, few players have been respected more than McCrary because of his toughness and relentless will. Knee injuries forced him to retire in August 2003, and he received a send-off unlike any other in Ravens history.

In attendance were Newsome, Billick, owner Art Modell, and about 20 players who asked special permission to attend. At that time, the Ravens held special events in a double-wide trailer in the back of the facility, and it was standing-room only for McCrary. The emotions were so high that defensive line coach Rex Ryan burst into tears and was momentarily unable to talk because he was too choked up.

"There's nobody like this guy," Modell said.

McCrary was placed in the team's Ring of Honor in October 2004.

Tony Siragusa

The Ravens may not have reached the Super Bowl if not for this self-proclaimed "fat guy" from New Jersey belly-slamming a quarterback.

Tony Siragusa, known as a run-stuffer throughout his career, took out Oakland Raiders quarterback Rich Gannon by driving him into the turf and separating his left shoulder. The All-Pro quarterback was never the same.

"I saw Rich's eyes roll back," Siragusa said. "He got every pound of my fat ass on him."

Siragusa ran a stunt with defensive end Michael McCrary, who slanted inside, and Siragusa looped outside. The 342-pound defensive tackle had a clean shot at Gannon, knocking the quarterback off his feet and pancaking him to the ground.

"There's a lot of dead weight," defensive end Rob Burnett said. "I equate that to a piano falling off the Chrysler Building and hitting someone."

Did Siragusa intentionally try to hurt Gannon?

"I had a shot at him and I took it," Siragusa said. "He's the Raiders offense. If they don't have that guy, it's like not having your backbone."

The irrepressible and nearly irreplaceable defensive tackle dominated the spotlight off the field and sacrificed any chance of receiving it on the field. Statistics cannot prove his worth, and words cannot justly describe his character.

Across the NFL, he was known more for his nickname, "Goose," than for his punishing labor as the run-stopping foundation of the league's premier defense. The reward: countless knee surgeries and no Pro Bowl invitations.

But glitz and glamour never fit this grizzled 6-foot-3, 340-pound tough guy, capiche? Growing up in the cozy north-central New Jersey town of Kenilworth, Siragusa picked up a truck driver's foul mouth and a Sopranos attitude.

He hunts, fishes, and rides Harleys. He hosted a weekly radio show where he was rude, lewd, and charismatic all in the same hour.

Siragusa, though, swallowed that ego when he snapped on the helmet. He clawed and scratched out a selfless personal mission each game.

He willingly accepted the job of occupying double teams so All-Pro middle linebacker Ray Lewis had the freedom to roam and clean up the tackles. A high school state wrestling champion, Siragusa understood how to use leverage to take on the blocks as well as fight through them for the tackle when teams tried to block him with one lineman.

"It never really bothered me to get respect from people other than the people that I played with," Siragusa said. "I consider myself the ultimate team player."

Teammates will remember Siragusa for his notorious pranks.

There was a time when some of the younger players made a big pot of cocoa in the training room and Siragusa saw an opportunity to spike it with laxative before practice. It didn't take long to see his trickery go to work, as players continually rushed off the field.

"They say there is a person like you everywhere, but I believe God made one Goose with that personality," Ravens defensive tackle Larry Webster said. "Goose says what's on his mind. He's a fun guy to be around. He doesn't hold any punches. So if you take it the wrong way, you take it the wrong way."

For his radio show, Siragusa once asked receiver Patrick Johnson and fullback Obafemi Ayanbadejo to be guests. There was an ulterior motive.

Siragusa apparently thought his teammates needed help on their touchdown dances and had some strippers appear to show them some moves.

"He gets on every one of them, but he would have any one of their backs," said Rex Ryan, who was Siragusa's defensive line coach. "They know they can count on Goose. No matter what the situation, that they can look over and say, 'I want Tony Siragusa in my corner.' And he'd be there."

Siragusa's commitment to his team was apparent in 2000, when he was blocked, fell to the ground, and couldn't feel part of his body. His mother came running down from the stands and his older brothers sprinted to the locker room, where a golf cart had moved the motionless big man.

"From my head down, I couldn't move," Siragusa said. "It was the scariest thing that's happened to me in my life."

The medical staff told Siragusa he had to at least have an MRI to make sure there wasn't spinal damage. He had a bruised spine, and he was advised not to go back. But he didn't heed that advice.

Said Siragusa: "[Defensive line] coach Rex Ryan came up to me and said 'You've got a family. Don't go back out there.' I said, 'You're my family, too. I've got to do this.'"

Beating the odds was the story of Siragusa's football career.

"I remember as a young player in Indy, the doctor examined my knee and he said, 'You don't have an ACL.' I said, 'You're a good doctor for noticing,'" Siragusa recalled. "He told me that he's seen it before and players last two or three years. I remembered that. Many years later, I thanked the doctor for motivating me like he did."

Rob Burnett

Would the Ravens have had a record-setting defense without its Dalai Lama? They were close to finding out.

Defensive end Rob Burnett was on the verge of retiring a year before the Ravens' championship 2000 season. He was in a contract year and believed he wouldn't be offered another one.

The 1997 and 1998 seasons were difficult on him because he had torn ligaments in his right knee and they hadn't healed all the way. He estimated that his leg was at 70 percent for those seasons.

Not only did Burnett stick it out, but also he was the tone-setter for a defense that will be remembered as one of the best in NFL history. Burnett didn't just sack quarterbacks that first month of the 2000 season. He obliterated them.

The biggest hit laid on a quarterback by that season's Ravens defense came against the Cincinnati Bengals in Week 4, when Burnett rocketed high into Akili Smith's chest and dropped him like he'd been standing in the path of a semi on the freeway. It's one of the few times when Baltimore fans collectively gasped when a player on another team was drilled into the ground.

"I try to play hard and fair. I talked to him after the game, and I'm glad he was all right because I'm not trying to hurt anybody," Burnett said. "I was very upset when that happened."

How quickly Burnett got there was just as impressive as the devastation of the blow. For Smith, one minute he's taking the snap from center and the next he's laying face-first in the turf.

Ironically, the play call was for a three-step drop, which is designed to beat the expected blitz.

"I don't know what happened," said Smith, who was knocked out of the game with a concussion. "I just remember getting hit. My stomach hurt. Throat hurt. It was a pretty good shot."

Three weeks earlier, Burnett was named AFC Defensive Player of the Week after the Ravens' season-opening 16-0 win at Pittsburgh. He pushed the Ravens to their first points of the season when he leveled Steelers quarterback Kent Graham in the first quarter, forcing a fumble that gave Baltimore the ball in the red zone.

"The Pittsburgh hit was pretty good, too, because he took two steps and jumped into Kent Graham," Ravens middle linebacker Ray Lewis said. "The impact of Smith's hit was a great hit, but it was kind of close. It wasn't a 20-yard run and hit."

By the end of September, he recorded 25 tackles, 4.5 sacks for 24 yards lost, one interception, two passes defensed, and three forced fumbles. He became the first Raven to win AFC Defensive Player of the Month.

The Ravens certainly took their cue that season from Burnett, the most underrated leader on a defense that had the likes of Lewis and safety Rod Woodson. Inside the locker room, few were more admired than Burnett.

"He's the Dalai Lama of the defensive line," defensive tackle Tony Siragusa said. "He's the ideal professional. When you're in this league eight, nine, 10 years, and you're a veteran like myself, it's harder to go around the locker room and gain wisdom from people. But Rob is one of the few guys that I do [learn from]."

Burnett had been there from the beginning, when the Ravens defense ranked 30th in 1996 and gave up 27.6 points per game. When the 2000 regular season was over, Burnett had a career-high 10.5 sacks and the Ravens recorded three shutouts.

"I'm not going out there to pitch a shutout," Burnett said. "I'm not Pedro Martinez."

The Ravens defense did pitch a shutout in the Super Bowl. He contributed four tackles and a sack for a defense that held the New York Giants offense to 152 total yards and no points. The Giants avoided an official shutout by scoring on a kickoff return for a touchdown.

It didn't take Burnett long to realize that he was going to earn his first ring at the age of 32.

"When the score was 7-0," Burnett said, "I was telling people, 'That's enough.' We're low maintenance in Baltimore. We only need seven, or 10 [points]. I was telling people it was over. I was saying it right to the cameras."

Burnett savored a personal triumph that would've eluded him if he had called it quits.

"Seems like I made the right decision," Burnett said. "Seems like some of my premonitions and hopes I had for this team have come to pass. . . . For something like this to happen, really I didn't bank on it. I was hoping, but it makes it so much sweeter."

Peter Boulware

Peter Boulware was the Ravens' "Lethal Weapon" in 1999.

That's what beat reporters used to affectionately call Boulware, a play on the Mel Gibson movies where the character's shoulder routinely popped out of place. Boulware sometimes teased them back, playfully slamming his shoulder in lockers.

Boulware's shoulder first became separated on the final day of the spring minicamp that year, and it looked like his season was over before it began. Except Boulware did not sit. He played every game. He played with a harness on his shoulder that essentially made him a one-armed player against 300-pound blockers. Or, in his case, a one-armed bandit who finished with 10 sacks and truly earned a trip to the Pro Bowl.

"He was a true warrior," defensive end Michael McCrary said. "Ninety-nine percent of the people in this league would have went ahead and had surgery with that injury. I don't know many people who would have played a season with one arm. And for him to accumulate those types of statistics and be a factor is amazing. That's the only word to describe what he did that year."

Boulware lost 10 pounds that year because he couldn't do weight work. He had to use his feet and increased quickness more than ever.

As expected, the shoulder popped out during games, too. Boulware was in so much pain during a November game in Cleveland that it took four people to hold him down to sedate him. He refused to quit even though he was limited to pass-rushing situations.

"My family wanted me to give it up and have surgery. They said it wasn't worth what I was going through. They were just looking out for my safety," Boulware said. "I prayed about it and said, 'Lord show me what to do.' And I felt, in my heart of hearts, it felt like the Lord was telling me to play and he'd make a way for me to get through it."

Boulware added, "You may call me crazy now, but I wouldn't give up that season for anything. It taught me some things about myself. I was facing an impossible situation and I was still able to overcome it. Those are lessons in life that you cannot learn without adversity."

With a combination of stunning quickness, relentless pursuit, and indisputable courage, Boulware finished with 70 sacks in his nine-year career.

He was the No. 4 overall pick in the 1997 draft and quickly became a feared linebacker in the league. A four-time Pro Bowl performer, he recorded sacks in 57 games and against 37 quarterbacks (Boulware sacked quarterback Mark Brunell 15 times).

"Peter was such a warrior," coach Brian Billick said. "I think of Peter Boulware because he had that look in his eye. His whole world was getting to that quarterback."

A major reason why the Ravens drafted Boulware was the tenacity of defensive coordinator Marvin Lewis.

As defensive coordinator for the Ravens in 1997, Lewis essentially staked out general manager Ozzie Newsome's office that April to make the case for drafting Boulware. Lewis had personally worked out Boulware and was convinced he could make the switch from a defensive end at Florida State to a linebacker in the NFL.

"Peter brought unbelievable physical talent and skills to the Ravens, and those were surpassed by his drive and his work ethic," Lewis said.

Boulware was the first Ravens player to win an NFL award, being named the league's Defensive Rookie of the Year in 1997, when he recorded 11.5 sacks. His best statistical season came in 2001, when he led the AFC with 15 sacks.

There were always two Boulwares with the Ravens.

"I appreciated the one Peter," Billick said, "but I loved the other one on game day."

Off the field, he was a loyal family man and a devout Christian. Boulware didn't believe in pre-marital sex, which led to some good-natured ribbing in the locker room. Still, most teammates had an immense amount of respect for Boulware because he was firm in his beliefs. Boulware was a regular at team Bible study and on the circuit for mentoring kids.

The Boulware on the field played with a nasty mean streak. Team officials once joked that Boulware was the all-time leader in personal fouls as well as sacks. In 2002, he was penalized for a personal foul in four straight games.

"I try to be a good Christian guy off the field. Once I got inside those lines, I can do anything I want to do," Boulware said. "To be good and to give it everything you have, you put all your emotions into it. I wanted to be the type of guy that when I walked off the field, everything was left there. Hopefully, that's the way I played it."

In November 2006, Boulware became the first player who played his entire career with the Ravens to get inducted into the team's Ring of Honor.

Duane Starks

The smallest starter on the Ravens' record-setting defense took a stand in the Super Bowl run.

Labeled the weak link of the record-setting defense in the regular season, 5-foot-9 cornerback Duane Starks made quarterbacks pay for attacking him in the postseason. He led the Ravens with three interceptions in the playoffs, which included a memorable highlight in the Super Bowl.

With the Ravens leading the Giants 10-0 in the third quarter, Starks picked off Kerry Collins and ran 49 yards for a touchdown. This critical turnover was just as much about anticipation as redemption.

Starks studied film in the two weeks leading up to the Super Bowl and found something. Collins was tipping his passes. When he dropped back to pass, if he was throwing off a three-step drop, he would hop on the second step.

"If you take one step and hop," Starks said, "the ball has to come out."

It proved to be valuable counterintelligence for Starks. As soon as he saw the hop, he broke on a Collins pass to wide receiver Amani Toomer.

"The only thing I could say was, 'Just catch the ball,'" Starks said.

There was no such confidence earlier in the year. In Week 2 against Jacksonville, Starks had a role in allowing touchdown catches of 45, 43, and 40 yards to the Jaguars' Jimmy Smith. Each one seemed like a replay, with Starks there to make the play but misjudging the ball at the very end.

Starks took the adversity head-on. After the rough game against the Jaguars, he stood in front of his locker and didn't leave until every reporter had asked a question.

Still, the general consensus was Starks went from being a first-round pick in 1998 to the worst starter on the Ravens' defense.

"I took that criticism very personal," Starks said. "It only strengthened me. Maybe I needed it, maybe I didn't. I just maintained my focus on what I had to do and didn't worry about what other people were saying about me. I just had to take the lead and knew what I had to get done."

There were times when he peeked in the backfield at the quarterback, which made him lose track of the receivers. Then, there were occasions on the deep throws when he would lunge out for the ball, trying to catch it at a high point rather than taking the extra step to get the best angle.

Quarterbacks didn't hide the fact that they had more reason to avoid looking to Chris McAlister's side of the field.

"Teams started to throw at him," Baltimore safety Rod Woodson said. "He either had to step up or step out. He stepped up."

Starks' first big statement came in the 2000 AFC Championship victory at Oakland. One of the game's heroes, Starks intercepted two passes and made five tackles.

The first interception led to a Ravens field goal. Not in the field of vision when quarterback Bobby Hoying released the ball, Starks kept receiver James Jett in front of him, then raced up after Jett made his break on the comeback route.

The second interception answered a Ravens fumble in their own territory. Instead of breaking too early on a deep pass to Andre Rison, Starks stayed in stride with Rison before undercutting him for the interception.

"Big-time players make big-time plays in big games," Starks said. "It's very rewarding for a guy who's been through what I've been through. No one believed in me."

Starks never lost faith, something that runs in the family. It so happens that his father, Willie, is a minister.

"The fact that he played so well was probably sort of redemption for him," coach Brian Billick said, "although I hesitate to use that term because I don't know if he needed any vindicating."

Starks signed a five-year, $23 million contract with the Arizona Cardinals as a free agent after the 2001 season, a deal the cap-strapped Ravens couldn't match. General manager Ozzie Newsome said Starks was the player he regretted losing the most in the team's 2002 rebuilding offseason.

Jamie Sharper

On the Ravens' record-setting defense, Jamie Sharper was the "other" linebacker.

Ray Lewis had more tackles than Sharper. Peter Boulware had more sacks than him. Lewis and Boulware both went to Pro Bowls and received national recognition.

Sharper? He was the understated playmaker on a defense that was full of big names and bigger personalities.

"One of the reasons our defense was No. 1 was because Jamie stepped it up and just really played like an All-Pro player," Boulware said. "When he started playing like that, our defense was hard to beat."

Sharper's development came from years of hard work and some tough love from defensive coordinator Marvin Lewis. In an article on the Ravens linebackers before the 1998 season, Lewis made the point that Sharper had "further to go than the other two."

Later that season, the tension between them peaked after Sharper blew back-to-back pass coverage assignments, which led to a big play in the Ravens' 14-13 loss in San Diego. As Sharper slumped on the bench, Lewis screamed at him, asking if he belonged with the Chargers. An upset Sharper tossed a cup of Gatorade on Lewis. Players watched in disbelief as Lewis ignored it.

"I didn't care. That's the reaction I wanted," Marvin Lewis said that season. "I wanted him [mad], because I was and so were the rest of the guys. So be it. When he doesn't care, that's when we have a problem. Jamie hasn't always agreed with what I've communicated to him, but we've come light years. I've got him on the same page with me."

Sharper never spoke out about being tormented by Lewis or complained about being overshadowed by his teammates, even though he was a more consistent player than Boulware.

His play elevated to another level toward the end of the magical 2000 season. He was named AFC Defensive Player of the Week after returning an interception 45 yards to set up the game-winning touchdown in a 13-7 win at Arizona. He also caused a fourth-quarter fumble at the Ravens' five-yard line, one of his team-leading five forced fumbles that season.

In the AFC Championship Game, Sharper led the team with nine tackles. He also had two sacks and intercepted a pass at the Ravens' two-yard line to stall a fourth-quarter drive and seal a 16-3 win at the Oakland Raiders.

In the Ravens' 34-7 Super Bowl win, he picked off a pass that was tipped by Ray Lewis.

"If he were anywhere else, he'd be the star linebacker," tight end Shannon Sharpe said repeatedly during his last two seasons in Baltimore.

The lasting image of Sharper is the one from *Sports Illustrated's* Super Bowl cover in 2001. With the headline "Baltimore Bullies," there's a photo of Sharper flying toward Kerry Collins and clawing at the facemask of the New York Giants quarterback.

Sharper received a blow-up of the photo that made him, for that moment, not the "other" linebacker. But Sharper keeps it inside a closet along with some other NFL mementos.

"That's Ray's team. Getting attention or notoriety never bothered me," Sharper said. "All I ever wanted was a ring. That's what was important to me in Baltimore."

In five years with the Ravens (1997–2001), Sharper started every game but one. He finished among the top three tacklers on the team in his final three seasons, totaling over 100 tackles each time.

His run with the Ravens ended after the 2001 season when they let him go to the Houston Texans in the expansion draft. The Ravens couldn't afford him in their salary-cap purge that offseason.

A staph infection in his right knee forced Sharper's retirement in 2006. He and his brother Darren, a safety who won a Super Bowl with the 2009 New Orleans Saints, are one of five pairs of siblings ever to have earned championship rings.

The Billick Era
(1999–2007)

Chapter 4

INSPIRATION FOR A TITLE

Brian Billick

Brian Billick turned around the Ravens' franchise, injecting the perennial losers with swagger and defiance.

He was the coach who proclaimed that the Ravens had to go into a playoff game in Tennessee "screaming like a banshee." He was the one who scolded hundreds of reporters at the Super Bowl for hounding Ray Lewis about his double-murder case from a year prior.

So, how did the leader of the NFL's bold and brash bullies soak in his triumph at the Super Bowl? With a paralyzing rush of anxiety.

It happened after Billick pulled himself away from the Ravens' party at 6 a.m. and went back to his hotel suite to refresh himself.

"In the shower, I had, for a lack of a better word, a panic attack," Billick said. "It was like, 'Oh shit, where do I go from here?' I had won a Super Bowl in my second year and all that's doing is setting the bar, that if you don't repeat this thing pretty quick, they're going to run your ass out of town even quicker. It eventually passed."

A couple hours later, Billick had to go speak in front of the media for his day-after press conference. NFL commissioner Paul Tagliabue sat down with Billick, who had called reporters "ambulance chasers" earlier in the week, and asked him to take a professorial approach this time.

"Kevin [Byrne, the Ravens vice president of public relations] and I looked at each other like, 'Well, that ain't going to happen," Billick said.

When he stood at the podium, Billick said, "If you thought I was arrogant before—whoa! Wait until you get a load of me now."

That's the Billick everyone knew. That's the Billick his players respected and admired.

Before Billick arrived in January 1999, the Ravens were 16-31-1 in the club's first three seasons under coach Ted Marchibroda. The team never finished higher than fourth in the AFC Central.

In nine seasons with Billick, the Ravens reached the playoffs four times, capturing their first Super Bowl title in the 2000 season and winning the AFC North twice (2003 and 2006).

The Ravens didn't just win. They told you all week that they were going to win. Just like their coach, the players talked trash and backed it up.

Credit: Tom Uhlman

"I think Brian's personality probably fits more the players on this team than probably any other coach's personality fits their team," tight end Shannon Sharpe said.

Combative. Conceited. Condescending.

These are all words that have been used to describe Billick. One media member at the Super Bowl once asked what was bigger: Billick's ego or Tony Siragusa's waistline?

That was the outside perception, and to a degree, Billick and the Ravens projected that image. Inside Ravens' headquarters, the directive was much different.

One reason why Billick chose to become head coach of the Ravens over the Cleveland Browns was the talent on the roster. In 1998, the year before Billick was hired, the Ravens had as many Pro Bowl players (six) as wins.

When Billick came the next year, he basically challenged the team to check their egos before leaving their first meeting. He asked them: Do you want to go to the Pro Bowl or the Super Bowl?

Then, in what was a cruel twist of fate, Billick himself had to check his ego to guide the Ravens to the Super Bowl. This wasn't the most explosive offense in NFL history. He created that two years earlier when he was the offensive coordinator of the Minnesota Vikings.

To win with the Ravens, Billick had to disregard everything he had grown to believe about successful offenses. He had to adopt a conservative, ball-control mentality. He basically had to write the book on how to win ugly in the NFL.

"It did feel like I was going over to the dark side," Billick said, "but the force was with me."

His vision of the offense changed when the Ravens didn't score a touchdown in five games, going 0-for-October. "The Drought" turned a 3-1 team into a 5-4 one, and the Ravens could've easily unraveled.

Billick's greatest achievement was keeping together a team that couldn't have been more splintered, with a defense that posted shutouts and an offense that continually got shut out of the end zone.

"I've got to be able to do something. There's something I can do to change this. That's my job, my responsibility," Billick said. "But you couldn't beat [the offensive players] up. Their confidence was going to be so fragile. The other part of that is the defense needs to know you recognize the problem. They want to see something done."

The decision that changed the Ravens' season was benching quarterback Tony Banks at midseason and turning to the maligned Trent Dilfer. "Manage the offense," Billick said. "Be patient; be efficient," he implored. "Let the relentless defense win the game."

Billick took the ball out of the air and put it in the hands of rookie running back Jamal Lewis, turning to Sharpe or special teams and defense for the big plays the Ravens needed.

Once the touchdown drought ended, the Ravens went on another streak—a winning one. The challenge for Billick now was figuring out a way to keep a team with a 7-4 record focused, and this is where the idea of his infamous ban was born.

There was to be no letup in preparation, no relaxing of work ethic, no mention of the P-word, as in playoffs. For a franchise that had never come close to qualifying for the postseason, Billick's message was clear: you had to earn the right to say it.

"The kangaroo court is officially in session, and I am the Supreme Court judge in this matter," Billick said at the time. "There will be fines for anybody in this organization—anybody in this organization—that mentions the P-word. We can kind of have fun with that, but believe me, the fines will be legitimate and they will be severe, and the players will be made aware of that, as is everybody else in the building. Because it's important for us to recognize that's exactly where we're at."

The motivated Ravens shut out the Dallas Cowboys, 27-0, and routed the Cleveland Browns, 44-7, the following week. It wasn't until the Ravens dominated the San Diego Chargers, 24-3, that the ban on the P-word was lifted. The Ravens clinched the franchise's first playoff berth that day, and Billick surprised the players with another announcement.

"Men, the time is here. It's time to go to a Super Bowl," Billick told his players in the locker room following the game.

Dilfer later said that this was "the most genius move" Billick ever made.

"This set the stage, and I'm so glad he showed the balls to do it," Dilfer said. "I had just left Tampa where all we talked about was, 'Let's just get into the playoffs and let's see what happens.' Bullcrap. Let's go try and win the Super Bowl."

The Ravens' Super Bowl run included Billick's signature moment. Minutes before the Ravens kicked off at Tennessee in the AFC divisional playoff game, the Titans ran clips of his incendiary quotes on the big screen at Adelphia Coliseum.

The Titans thought they were gaining an edge. Instead, it gave one to the Ravens. As the video played, Billick stalked the sideline in a fury, telling his players they had to cover his back. When the Ravens did score against the Titans to tie the game at 7-7, Billick was captured on television turning to the Tennessee bench and mouthing a rather forceful expletive.

"Ray Lewis said, 'I love my coach because he talks you-know-what like we do,'" Sharpe said. "I love Brian for the fact that he doesn't talk all that gibberish you don't want to hear. I like Brian's braggadocious attitude because I'm like that."

After the game, Billick defended his team's swagger by exclaiming: "When you go into the lion's den, you don't tippy-toe in. You carry a spear. You go in screaming like a banshee and say, 'Where's the son of a bitch?'"

Over a decade later, this remains the most famous quote from Billick's time as Ravens head coach. He still remembers why he said it, too.

The Titans were considered the favorite to go to the Super Bowl from the AFC that season, and earlier that season, the Ravens had become the first visiting team to ever win at Tennessee's home stadium. There were rumblings heading into that playoff game in Nashville that the Titans thought it was classless the way the Ravens constantly "woofed" about it.

"That's where I kind of burn up and go, 'Wait a minute now, this is the team to beat. This is the team that *Sports Illustrated* called the best in football on its cover," Billick said. "Well, bullshit. You don't go into that environment with a hemming and hawing attitude and with that humble 'ah shucks, we're just lucky to be here' mentality."

So, where did Billick come up with the famous "banshee" expression?

"I'm sure I stole it from some place," Billick said. "I can't for the life of me tell you where."

Billick never coached the Ravens back to the pinnacle of the NFL, but he did put together some remarkable seasons.

In 2001, he took the defending Super Bowl champions to the divisional round despite losing Jamal Lewis in training camp. The following year, he led the Ravens to a 7-9 record with a team featuring 19 rookies, the most on any team since the league went to a 53-man roster in 1993.

Billick won his first division title in 2003, but he missed the playoffs the next two seasons. That forced him into making another pivotal move in the middle of the 2006 season. He fired his offensive coordinator and good friend Jim Fassel and took over the play-calling duties.

The Ravens averaged 18.3 points per game with Fassel as offensive coordinator; in going 9-1 with Billick calling the plays, Baltimore averaged 24.3 points.

"We knew the kind of heat he put upon himself," offensive tackle Jonathan Ogden said. "He was saying, 'I think if something is going to happen, it's going to be my fault. If I'm going to be out of here, it's going to be because of me.' That says accountability to us."

The Ravens earned the AFC's No. 2 seed but was bounced in their first playoff game by the Indianapolis Colts.

The following season, just months after signing a new four-year contract, Billick endured the worst season of his NFL coaching career. He lost his top two quarterbacks (Steve McNair and Kyle Boller), his leading receiver from the previous season (tight end Todd Heap) and both starting cornerbacks (Chris McAlister and Samari Rolle) to significant injuries throughout the year. The Ravens lost nine straight games before beating the Pittsburgh Steelers in the season finale.

Eventually, he lost the team. Billick was fired December 31, 2007, a move that floored him.

"That was probably the most embarrassing thing to me, not being more aware," Billick said. "It wasn't out of blind ignorance. I had sat down with Ozzie [Newsome, general manager] and Steve [Bisciotti] a week earlier and our conversations were totally revolved around steps I needed to take, who I was going to interview for the offensive coordinator's job, and what we needed to do. It was all about what we needed to do going forward."

When Billick walked into Ravens headquarters a day after the season ended, he was going to begin his interviews for offensive coordinator and stopped by to talk to Newsome, where he first learned the news.

"I think Steve's going in a different direction," Newsome told Billick.

Newsome thought there was a chance that Bisciotti would change his mind. That didn't happen, and Billick knew it the instant he sat down with Bisciotti for the last time as the Ravens coach.

"With Steve, I could tell immediately, even though Ozzie thought that maybe we can talk him back; I could tell the resolve in Steve," Billick said. "He had made a decision. There was no going back. He said, 'Brian, I have too much respect for you and I care for you too much to sit here and tell you on a blow by blow why I'm doing this.' I thought, *Okay, if you don't want to say it, I definitely don't want to hear it.* So, we parted ways."

A day after he was fired, Billick came back to Ravens headquarters to clean out his office. Newsome asked him about potential coaching candidates.

"I don't want to take credit for it," Billick said, "but I believe I'm the one who first wanted to bring up John Harbaugh."

Billick knew about Harbaugh from his connection with Philadelphia Eagles coach Andy Reid. Just 19 days after Billick was let go, the Ravens hired Harbaugh as the third head coach in franchise history.

Shannon Sharpe

No player in Ravens history has had a bigger impact in such a brief period of time than tight end Shannon Sharpe.

Former team president David Modell called Sharpe the biggest free-agent signing in the team's history and believes the Ravens wouldn't have captured their first Lombardi Trophy without him. There's an old adage in football that no team is one player away from winning a Super Bowl, but Sharpe was that *one player* for the Ravens.

In his two seasons in Baltimore, the Ravens went 22-10 in the regular season and won five games in the playoffs. Sharpe's big personality and big mouth instilled much-needed confidence at the most critical times of the game. His big plays defined his leadership and proven track record in the postseason.

Landing Sharpe in February 2000 seemed too good to be true. It had nothing to do with Ravens general manager Ozzie Newsome being skeptical about Sharpe's production. He just couldn't believe the Broncos would part with a perennial Pro Bowl player who had such a strong presence in the locker room.

"I was at the Super Bowl and Ray Lewis told me Shannon would like to come and play for us," Newsome said. "I said, 'Yeah, right.'"

It turned out that Sharpe needed the Ravens. Denver Broncos coach Mike Shanahan thought the tight end was going to be too expensive, considering that he would be 32 at the time and had played in just five games during the 1999 season because of a fractured left clavicle.

The Ravens not only needed a productive tight end but a player who wore two Super Bowl rings. Sharpe is about winning, first and foremost, and he taught the Ravens about clutch play in his second game with the team.

In Week 2 of the 2000 season, Sharpe caught the winning, 29-yard touchdown pass from Tony Banks that lifted the Ravens to a 39-36 victory over the Jacksonville Jaguars.

It was the first time in Ravens history that the offense pulled out a victory in the final two minutes. In fact, all clutch victories in Ravens history date back to Sharpe.

"We had a lot of young players at the time," Newsome said. "Shannon became a leader, especially on the offensive side of the ball, because he had been to Super Bowls, and he could tell those guys what they needed to do to win."

Sharpe carried the Ravens offense in the franchise's first trip to the playoffs, tucking the team under his arm just like he did with that short Trent Dilfer pass in the AFC Championship Game and running 96 yards for a touchdown.

That play still stands as the longest completion in NFL playoff history. And, in usual Sharpe fashion, he didn't do it quietly.

In a scoreless game in Oakland, the Ravens took the field and Sharpe told his teammates in the huddle, "We're going to be on 'SportsCenter' tonight. You all just watch." Three plays later, on a third-and-18 at his own four-yard line with the rowdy Raiders crowd screaming in his ear, Sharpe caught a short pass on a slant, slipped out of a tackle, and scored what would be the game's only touchdown.

"Great players can always back up their talk," Dilfer said.

The key to the play, which was called "Rip Double Slant," was that it caught the Raiders blitzing. Sharpe caught the pass from Dilfer at the 10-yard line, eluded strong safety Marquez Pope, and raced to the end zone.

"I was trying to find the Jumbotron so I could see where guys are coming from. But it was in the corner and I couldn't see it, so I just kept running and looking back," Sharpe said of his only reception in the game. "[Ravens receiver] Patrick Johnson scared me because he almost tripped me twice."

Flanked by Johnson, Sharpe stayed a couple paces ahead of his closest pursuers, free safety Anthony Dorsett and cornerback Eric Allen. Dorsett made a desperate dive inside the five-yard line, but couldn't stop Sharpe.

"I consider myself pretty fast, but it's like, I'm slow. I'm taking a long time to get to the end zone,'" Sharpe said. "I didn't realize it was that far. It seemed like I'd never get to the end zone."

Whenever the Ravens needed a big play in the playoffs, Sharpe was the one who delivered it. Some catches, like the one in Oakland, made you wonder whether it was luck or simply fate.

In the Ravens' first-ever playoff game, Sharpe scored on a 58-yard touchdown pass, off two deflections no less, in a 21-3 win over his former team, the Denver Broncos.

Sharpe was supposed to run a 10-yard hitch route, but he noticed the Broncos playing a deep zone and decided to cut off his pattern by five yards. That's the only reason Sharpe was in that area to catch a ball that went off the hands of the Ravens' Jamal Lewis and bounced off the chest of Denver's Terrell Buckley.

"I was at the wrong place at the right time," Sharpe said.

In the divisional round game at Tennessee the following week, Sharpe's 56-yard catch-and-run set up the Ravens' only touchdown in a 24-10 victory over the Titans.

"I'm fast. I'm bad fast," Sharpe said. "I'm telling you I've got Randy Moss speed. OK, maybe not Randy Moss. Maybe Spanish moss."

In the playoffs that year, Sharpe caught just five passes, but they totaled 225 yards (45-yard average) and three touchdowns. The extraordinary run of postseason big gains surprised even Sharpe.

"I've never done anything like it, never," he said. "I don't know what it is. The end result is—and this is one thing I've always taken from Mike Shanahan—that when you're on the road, you get one or two opportunities to make a big play. And if you make a big play, nine times out of 10, you'll be able to kill a team."

The following season, Sharpe broke Newsome's NFL record for most catches and receiving yards for a tight end. He did it while wearing Newsome's No. 82 on his jersey, and the game was stopped so Newsome could come out on the field and congratulate Sharpe.

Unfortunately for Sharpe, his achievement came in a 27-17 loss to the Cleveland Browns.

"I've said all along that no individual goal supersedes a win. I'm a firm believer in that," Sharpe said. "Yeah, I'm pleased with the record, my family was here, but you can't do what we did and win a ballgame."

The Ravens lost in the divisional round of the playoffs in Pittsburgh that season, and Sharpe was among the many veterans released in the team's 2002 salary-cap purge.

Sharpe was upset initially by being let go by the Ravens, but he has since come to terms with the decision.

"I don't think anyone associated with the Ravens for those two years has any regrets," Sharpe said.

After Sharpe was released, the Ravens didn't win another playoff game for the next six years.

Trent Dilfer

The Ravens' first Super Bowl–winning quarterback was signed as an afterthought.

The Ravens never expected Trent Dilfer to play; Tony Banks was their quarterback. Head coach Brian Billick made it clear that Dilfer wasn't competing for the starting job, and short of an injury, nothing was going to change that.

Dilfer had other plans.

"I never doubted that I would be the quarterback for that football team," Dilfer said. "I was 100 percent sure."

Dilfer's confidence was shocking considering he was ripped more than any quarterback in the league during his six seasons with the Tampa Bay Buccaneers.

It wasn't that the pain, which comes when fans boo you off fields and harass your family in a restaurant, suddenly disappeared. The emotional scars were still there, like the ones obtained when teammates took the songs that mocked Dilfer on local radio and played them in the weight room.

All of this just made Dilfer stronger, more humble, and a better teammate when he came to Baltimore. It knocked down an inflated ego and gave him the right mindset to quarterback this team, even though it took Banks' meltdown for anyone to realize it.

Six weeks after throwing a career-high five touchdown passes against the Jacksonville Jaguars, Banks flamed out with three interceptions in the third quarter against the Tennessee Titans at home.

Banks lost the game and his job. The Ravens were 5-3, but they had lost two straight games and didn't reach the end zone for four weeks in a row.

"We got to let Trent try to do something here," Billick told a dejected Banks after his third interception against the Titans. "We got to, Tony."

Dilfer lost his first start for the Ravens, but that would be his only one for the franchise. He won his next 11 games, a win streak that has never been duplicated in Ravens history.

In his second start, Dilfer ended the Ravens' touchdown drought with a pass to Brandon Stokley, a receiver he built a rapport with when they spent the first half of the season on the scout team together.

The time when teammates really embraced Dilfer was the following week at Tennessee. In the Ravens' biggest regular-season game of the season, Dilfer threw a fourth-quarter interception that was returned for a touchdown, a blunder that dogged him throughout his NFL career.

"I went into the huddle, and it was 10 guys looking at me with the belief that in the next 2.5 minutes we were going to do something special," Dilfer said. "I never had that in Tampa. Sometimes it was nine guys. Sometimes it was seven. Sometimes it was one."

Dilfer added, "To look in that huddle and see those people looking back at me, to me, was the defining moment of this team."

Trailing 23-17 with 2:18 remaining, Dilfer drove the Ravens 70 yards and completed the winning drive with a two-yard touchdown pass to Patrick Johnson.

It marked the Titans' first loss at Adelphia Coliseum and stamped the Ravens as a Super Bowl contender for the first time in their existence.

"Trent helped give us chemistry," tight end Shannon Sharpe said. "He would talk to everyone, even on defense, and jump around and when he made a mistake, he'd admit it even if someone else was at fault. He proved he could win—not by talking or passing for tons of yards but by leading. He cared about winning, not stats."

That became apparent in Week 15, when the Ravens were routing the San Diego Chargers, 24-3, and moved into the red zone with three minutes left in the game. Billick called a passing play, a move that most quarterbacks would appreciate to pad their numbers. Dilfer, though, suggested the Ravens run out the clock and celebrate the win, which clinched the Ravens' first playoff berth.

"Trent was the perfect quarterback for us for that Super Bowl run," Billick said. "When called upon to start, he threw himself into that role and pulled the leadership of the team back as a quarterback has to and didn't go out and try to manufacture a bunch of stats knowing that he was going to be a free agent."

Dilfer struggled just as much on the practice field as in games. According to a team official, Ray Lewis, Shannon Sharpe, and Rod Woodson asked Billick to replace Dilfer with Banks before the first playoff game. Billick told the players he couldn't because Dilfer had won seven straight games.

The ugly stats and frequent ugly passes fed the perception that the Ravens defense and special teams strapped Dilfer to the hood of the team bus on the way to the Super Bowl. He ranked 20th in the NFL in passer rating in the regular season and completed less than half of his passes in the postseason.

After he helped the Ravens beat the Oakland Raiders in the AFC Championship Game, Dilfer was called the worst quarterback to ever start a Super Bowl. He was dubbed "the accidental quarterback."

For the first time during Super Bowl week, this question was asked: "Do you think you'll be a starting quarterback next year?"

Dilfer handled it all with a self-deprecating humor that came across harsher than his toughest critic.

"Brian is an offensive genius, and never more so than this year," Dilfer said. "He's done something like he's never had to do before. Anybody can scheme people with Randy Moss and Cris Carter and score a bunch of points. It's pretty hard with Trent Dilfer as your quarterback."

Dilfer started the Super Bowl with a 38-yard touchdown strike to Brandon Stokley in the first quarter before surviving a couple of scares. With the Ravens ahead 7-0 in the second quarter, Dilfer threw an interception that was returned for a touchdown, but a holding penalty on the New York Giants erased his error.

In the third quarter, Dilfer hurt his left hand and had to go to the locker room for X-rays, which revealed he injured two fingers. He returned to the game after missing one drive.

"Maybe the significance of hoisting up the Lombardi [Trophy] with a bandaged hand is to achieve anything great, you have to go through a lot of pain," Dilfer said.

Dilfer won the Super Bowl on his old stomping grounds in Tampa despite only completing 12 of 25 passes for 153 yards.

"We all know I'm not Joe Montana," Dilfer said. "But for the rest of my life, I'll have this."

Dilfer's exit from the Ravens was just as historic as his triumph.

For one exhilarating moment, Dilfer had the dream quarterbacking job of his life. In the next moment, he had no job at all.

When the Ravens signed Elvis Grbac in free agency—39 days after the Ravens won the Super Bowl—Dilfer went down in history as the first quarterback to win the Super Bowl and lose his job before the next season.

Even though the Ravens failed to repeat, general manager Ozzie Newsome said the team made the right decision about not re-signing Dilfer.

"We understood what Trent did for us; he was a tough sucker with a presence in the huddle," Newsome said. "I am still a great leader, but I can't play on Sunday. It is still about making plays on Sunday."

Dilfer expressed years of bitterness about the Ravens not giving him the opportunity to come back and repeat. He directed most of his anger at Billick and, at one time, vowed never to speak to him again.

"I don't know that we would have done anything different," Billick said. "One of the biggest regrets that I have, for a player, is for Trent to have to go through that. He was the perfect guy at the perfect time for that Super Bowl in Baltimore and I'll always appreciate that.

The business side of this usually rears its head and it's unfortunate when it does."

Years later, Woodson contends the Ravens would have repeated if the decision-makers hadn't messed with the team chemistry.

"Trent Dilfer was a gutsy quarterback whose gritty mindset fit that team perfectly," Woodson said. "One hundred percent of the players wanted him back."

Others have a different version of how the offseason unfolded.

"It gets to be fuzzy math for some," wide receiver Qadry Ismail said. "How come everybody forgets that all of the leaders went up to Brian and said they didn't want Trent?"

Dilfer made two starts against the Ravens after that Super Bowl season and lost both times. Before his last start against them in 2007, he publicly apologized to Billick for the way he expressed his anger.

"I recognize they had a tough decision as an organization. I disagree with it still to this day," Dilfer said. "[But] just because I disagree with it doesn't mean I can't let it go."

Jermaine Lewis

In 2000, the Ravens handled all of the distractions from Ray Lewis' offseason legal drama. They overcame a frustrating touchdown drought. They persevered through a quarterback change in the middle of the season.

Then, two days after the Ravens clinched their first playoff berth in team history, another personal tragedy rocked the team. Geronimo, the son of returner Jermaine Lewis, was stillborn.

A routine doctor's visit revealed the umbilical cord had wrapped around the infant's neck and cut off his blood supply. Lewis' wife was eight months pregnant.

"That was as difficult a time for this team for the obvious reasons of the loss of a child, the affection we had for Jermaine," coach Brian Billick said. "It certainly leant a sense of appreciation for how tenuous this all is."

Lewis, the littlest Raven on the championship team at 5 feet 7, was looked upon as the little brother in the locker room. He was taken in the Ravens' first draft along with Jonathan Ogden and Ray Lewis, although Jermaine was selected four rounds after them.

Jermaine Lewis' speed was jaw dropping. He was the 1992 indoor athlete of the year by *Track & Field* magazine and he had the nation's second-fastest time in the 100-meter dash that same year.

Instead of being a world-class sprinter, Lewis became the NFL's best punt returner in 1997 and 1998. The reward was a new contract, but it led to a reality check. The next season, he averaged a career-low 7.9 yards per punt return.

"I'm just trying to get better instead of maybe thinking I've arrived," Lewis said at the time. "I haven't really arrived."

The 2000 season put everything in perspective for Lewis, personally as much as professionally. He averaged a career-best 16.1 yards on punt returns before learning the devastating news about his son's death.

Billick told Lewis to stay at home the next week and not make the cross-country trip to play the Arizona Cardinals. It was time to grieve and begin healing.

Lewis was ready to return for the regular-season finale, wanting to show his pain had a purpose. In his first game back, Lewis returned a punt 54 yards for a touchdown and ran back another 80 yards to tie the game with the New York Jets with five minutes left in the game.

Ravens quarterback Trent Dilfer actually shed a tear on Lewis' first touchdown, and he wasn't the only teammate in awe.

"When he ran the first one back, we said, 'Hey, it happened for a reason,'" safety Rod Woodson said. "When he ran the second one back, we're like, 'Hey, it's a godsend.'"

Before the Ravens' first Super Bowl, Jermaine Lewis wrote a message on his wristband. It read: Geronimo Lewis, Rest in Peace.

The rest of the football world would witness another acknowledgment of his son.

The New York Giants had just scored on a kickoff return, cutting the Ravens' lead in the Super Bowl to 17-7. The Giants had the momentum for exactly 18 seconds.

On the next kickoff, Lewis stepped up to make the catch, wiggled past a cluster of tacklers, bounced to his right, where he squeezed down the sideline after receiving blocks from Corey Harris and Sam Gash, and sprinted all the way to the end zone.

When Lewis crossed the goal line, he pointed to the sky, a private moment on football's biggest stage.

"I just wanted to put everything into closure and move on," Lewis said after the game. "I know he's looking out for me. I really already had a message [to him]. I was confident that I was going to score today."

For Lewis, it seemed like it was meant to be. No. 84 scored on an 84-yard touchdown.

It sucked the hope right out of the Giants and essentially sealed the first championship for the Ravens.

"There was nothing but emotion on the sideline," defensive tackle Tony Siragusa said. "He gave us all the strength we needed to finish the job."

Chapter 5

FINAL CHAMPIONSHIP PIECES

Chris McAlister

Chris McAlister was the final piece to the Ravens' championship puzzle or the most frustrating player in team history, depending on whom you ask.

McAlister was the top-rated defensive player on the Ravens' draft board in 1999. He was the top cornerback during an era when the Ravens dominated on defense. But he was also the team's top concern year after year, from his legal problems off the field to his divisive attitude in the locker room.

Brian Billick described coaching McAlister as "a full-time job."

"Unbelievable talent, time after time after time was self-destructive and tried to pull the team with him," Billick said. "We probably talked more in meetings about Chris McAlister and what we were going to do with him than any player in my entire time there and probably should have been more aggressive about cutting him loose."

Credit: Keith Allison

The reason why the Ravens kept McAlister around for 10 seasons was his ability to shut down the best receivers and take the ball to the end zone himself. A prototypical cornerback, he was strong enough to play bump-and-run, fast enough to cover man-to-man, and savvy enough to play in zone.

McAlister went to three Pro Bowls, although the talent was there to become a Hall of Fame cornerback. There were flashes of greatness, none more so than September 30, 2002, when he made his way into the NFL record books.

When Denver's Jason Elam came up short on a 57-yard field goal try at the end of the first half, McAlister fielded it deep in the end zone and hesitated before bringing it out. Following a crushing block by Ray Lewis, at the Baltimore five-yard line, McAlister broke to his left and easily outran the coverage. With Billick in pursuit on the sideline cheering him along, McAlister began waving the ball over his head and jogged the final 25 yards to the end zone.

McAlister's 107-yard return for a touchdown was the longest of any kind in NFL history. No pro had ever brought back a kickoff, punt, interception, field-goal attempt, or fumble farther.

"That's the way we practice it," McAlister said. "I watched and hung in the end zone and let my guys set up the wall. I got a hell of a block from Ray [Lewis], and we went with the wall. All I saw was purple jerseys and green until I hit the end zone."

This is the type of playmaking talent the Ravens envisioned when they used the 10th overall pick on McAlister in 1999, Billick's first draft as head coach. The Ravens were so confident that they would get either McAlister or cornerback Champ Bailey that they had already approached Rod Woodson about converting to a new position.

McAlister was considered one of the seven "special players" in that draft by the Ravens. After being drafted, McAlister attended his first minicamp before spending 10 days in jail for failing to pay a fine related to a petty theft charge a few years prior. This should've been a sign for the Ravens, who overlooked this youthful indiscretion at first.

"I knew [we'd be great] when we got Chris, and moved Rod to safety. I told Brian [Billick] this is the final piece of the puzzle," defensive coordinator Marvin Lewis said.

The Ravens defense was great with McAlister. He quickly emerged as a shutdown corner, and he let everyone know about it.

McAlister told reporters about how many games he didn't allow a reception and talked about how he had his sights on becoming the NFL's next Deion Sanders.

"I like to go out on a limb again and say I plan on re-creating this position again before I get out of the league," McAlister said in December 2000. "To be 6-1, 215 pounds and run a 4.2 40 [-yard dash] and cover anything that walks in a jersey or helmet. That's my goal before I get out of this league."

McAlister played confidently on the field, too. He scored seven touchdowns in his career, including a 98-yard interception return against the Jets' Vinny Testaverde in the 2000 regular-season finale. In the Super Bowl, McAlister intercepted a pass late in the half to end the best scoring opportunity for the New York Giants offense, jumping a route at the one-yard line.

As McAlister quieted receivers, his volume only increased. He made headlines by boasting that linebacker Ray Lewis had made Titans running back Eddie George "curl up like a baby" with a hit earlier in the 2000 season. He also told reporters that the defense only needed three points to beat the Giants in the Super Bowl.

"Art Modell told me I should be in movies," McAlister said, "but not silent movies, because I talk so much."

The off-the-field problems often overshadowed his play throughout his career.

McAlister was charged with misdemeanor possession of marijuana in 2000 and with driving under the influence in 2003. Charges were dropped in both cases. Later in 2003, McAlister broke curfew and missed the team meeting the next day during the Ravens' extended stay in San Diego. He was sent home and fined.

He questioned the Ravens' chemistry at the end of 2004, describing the locker room as "a little shifted." It seemed like McAlister embraced this bad-boy image, referring to himself as "the black sheep."

McAlister was known for drinking alone on road trips and regretted that decision on one visit to Pittsburgh, where he truly learned the extent of the Ravens-Steelers rivalry. He asked a valet for the closest bar and didn't notice he was in a gay bar until after he'd ordered a drink.

The Ravens' issues with McAlister continued after Billick was fired. In 2008, Harbaugh's first season, McAlister got burned for two touchdowns at Indianapolis in Week 6 and got benched the next game. Although there were discipline problems—he broke the team's dress code on a road trip and had three girls in his hotel room in another incident—Harbaugh said the decision to pull McAlister from the starting lineup was based on performance.

Even McAlister's release in February 2009 was rocky. McAlister said he talked with Harbaugh about coming back to the team and then walked across the hall to meet with general manager Ozzie Newsome, who told him that he was getting cut.

"This is a blind shot to me," McAlister said after being released. "The whole way it went down is probably the most disappointing thing to me. As far as mending fences, they can't be mended at this point."

Jamal Lewis

Drafting Jamal Lewis in the first round would define the Ravens' bruising image on offense. The pick was a surprise to everyone outside the Ravens' organization, except for the running back prodigy.

When the Ravens had the No. 5 overall pick in 2000, some thought the team would trade down. Others thought the Ravens would select a wide receiver or a running back like Thomas Jones, Shaun Alexander, or Heisman Trophy–winner Ron Dayne.

Why did Lewis have a feeling the Ravens would take him?

Two months before the draft, Lewis had a chat at the NFL Combine with Ravens running back coach Matt Simon about his weight.

"I want you to be at 230 pounds," Simon said.

Lewis, who was 240 pounds, simply responded, "OK."

Eight days later at his Pro Day, Lewis stepped on the scale and was 10 pounds lighter.

Lewis looked back at Simon, who winked and gave him a thumbs-up.

The selection of Lewis wasn't greeted with such approval by the national media. CNN college football analyst Trev Alberts described Lewis as "a horrible pick." *Sports Illustrated*'s Peter King wrote that the Ravens were "dumb" not to trade down and predicted Shaun Alexander would be a better running back than Lewis.

In the end, the Ravens were right. They have a Lombardi Trophy and a 2,000-yard season to show for it.

As a rookie, Lewis was the focal point of the Ravens' offense during their Super Bowl run, a punishing 1,300-yard rusher. And in 2003, one season after coming back from knee surgery, he was the NFL's Offensive Player of the Year.

During his six seasons with the Ravens, Lewis rolled up more than four miles of rushing yardage—7,801 yards, to be exact—with a majority of that coming from him running over tacklers and then running away from them.

"A force to be reckoned with," former Ravens head coach Brian Billick called him.

At the age of 21, Lewis carried the Ravens' offense in the franchise's first championship season. He was the workhorse back that doesn't exist in today's NFL, averaging 119.1 yards rushing and 26 carries during the Ravens' seven-game winning streak that ended the 2000 regular season.

In the Super Bowl, Lewis became the second rookie ever to rush for over 100 yards and the youngest player to score a touchdown when he stretched the ball across the goal line in the fourth quarter.

Lewis acknowledges now that he didn't savor the Super Bowl when he won it in his first season in the league.

"I thought it was easy," Lewis said. "I noticed year after year that this is not easy. It is very tough to go and beat out 32 teams to win a Super Bowl. Later on down in my career, is when I actually appreciated it more. I even appreciate it more now than I did then."

Lewis was invaluable to the Ravens, and that was underscored when the defending Super Bowl champions had to play without him. In one of the first practices of the 2001 training camp, Lewis tore the anterior cruciate ligament in his left knee and was done for the season.

The Ravens had to make do with the likes of Terry Allen and thoughts of what might have been.

"I think we won a Super Bowl in 2000 because we had Jamal Lewis, and I think the biggest reason why we didn't win it in 2001 is because Jamal got hurt," general manager Ozzie Newsome said. "If we would have had Jamal, we would not have had to put more pressure on [quarterback] Elvis Grbac. We would have been able to still have a balanced offense. When Jamal was not there because of the ACL tear in his leg, it forced a change in our offensive scheme. So I think if we would have had Jamal, we could have won back-to-back Super Bowls."

What Lewis remembers about that tragic moment is the Ravens had to keep practicing it over and over again because nose tackle Kelly Gregg repeatedly beat center Mike Flynn and threw off the play. With 10 minutes before practice ended, Lewis got hit by Gregg but was able to walk off the field without any help from trainers.

"It just so happened that he fell and turned my knee in some kind of way," Lewis said. "I thought that it was good because I could walk around and everything. When I got the [MRI] results back, I was like 'Wow!'"

The real jaw-dropping time of Lewis' career came in 2003, when he delivered a season for the ages just two years removed from that season-ending injury.

It began with a prediction, of sorts. Before the second game of the season, Lewis had a trash-talking session with Cleveland Browns linebacker Andra Davis over the phone after Billick made it known that the Ravens were going to hand it off to Lewis 30 times that week.

"If you get the ball 30 times, I'm going to have 30 tackles," Davis said.

Lewis responded, "If I get the ball 30 times, I'm going to have a career day."

Three days later, Lewis hammered his way to an NFL-record 295 yards, besting the previous mark by 17 yards.

"It was like Babe Ruth pointing to the fence before the home run," Billick said after the game.

On his first attempt, Lewis collected himself after nearly falling just past the line of scrimmage and bolted a team-record 82 yards for a touchdown. He had 105 yards after his second carry and 180 yards at halftime, when he first realized the record was within reach.

At halftime, offensive tackle Jonathan Ogden looked at Lewis and said, "Hey man, we can go for the record."

Lewis asked, "What record?"

Ogden replied, "The NFL single-game record. It's 274 yards or something."

Lewis would have surpassed 300 yards, but a 60-yard touchdown run was cut by 12 yards after receiver Marcus Robinson drew a penalty for holding.

"This is the most disgusting feeling I've had in my whole life," Browns safety Earl Little said. "He said what he said, he did it, and it's in the history books."

Lewis finished that season with 2,066 yards rushing, just 39 shy of Eric Dickerson's NFL record. He wasn't disappointed that he didn't break that mark because he knew he put everything into that season.

During practices, Lewis would finish plays by running 40 and 50 yards to the end zone. When he got home, he would get on the treadmill and jog.

"I just felt like a machine. I didn't feel anything," Lewis said. "Missing a year of football, you really find out how much you really love football and how much you really love this game and you really want to take back every minute. That moment, that season, I didn't want to leave no stone unturned."

Lewis would remain the Ravens' top running back for three more seasons, and although he never came close to matching that historic season, he never stopped producing. He surpassed 1,000 yards rushing in each of the 2004 and 2006 seasons before the Ravens cut him in February 2007 rather than pay him a $5 million roster bonus.

The Ravens attempted to re-sign him, but Lewis chose to go to the Cleveland Browns.

"They never brought in any linemen, and that was one of [the] things that I was really teed off at the Ravens," said Lewis, who only had one starting lineman (Ogden) blocking for him that was drafted in the first three rounds. "I was so worn out and beat up from being that punching bag. Honestly, I was ready to go."

Lewis came back to Baltimore in September 2012, three years after his final NFL carry, for his induction into the Ravens' Ring of Honor. He said he was "always a Raven at heart."

Qadry Ismail

Qadry Ismail can appreciate patience and perseverance every time he looks at his Super Bowl ring.

He went from being the Ravens' No. 1 wide receiver to an underutilized weapon during the team's championship run. This is what happens when an offense makes the switch from a strong-armed quarterback like Tony Banks to a game manager in Trent Dilfer.

There was frustration over the lack of passes thrown his way. There was anger over all the hard work in the offseason that had gone to waste. And there was astonishment over how the Ravens consistently won with Dilfer at quarterback.

"It was one of the most absolute rewarding years of my entire life," Ismail said, "and one of the most mentally draining years of my entire life."

This is a bold statement coming from a player who endured what he called his "wilderness experience."

Before joining the Ravens, he played for four NFL teams in three years. He spent 13 games on the Miami Dolphins' inactive list in one season. He went two years without a catch.

Opportunity came when Brian Billick, his coordinator when he was with the Minnesota Vikings, was searching for cheap prospects that he called his "trash heap" players.

"I knew what I was getting—unbelievable speed and good physical attributes," Billick said. "He'd drop about one out of every three balls. You just had to know that. That was OK because we had guys that either dropped two out of the three balls or couldn't get open in the first place."

The Ravens were getting by with the likes of Justin Armour, Patrick Johnson, and Jermaine Lewis. For the first time in his career, Ismail had an edge over his fellow receivers.

The biggest problem for Ismail was connecting with a Ravens quarterback. In 1999, Scott Mitchell lasted six quarters before being benched. Stoney Case went four starts before being pulled.

The Ravens finally turned to Banks, who instantly clicked with Ismail. In December 1999, Ismail amassed 258 receiving yards on six catches as the Ravens defeated the Pittsburgh Steelers, 31-24, their first-ever victory at Three Rivers Stadium. Ismail scored on touchdowns of 54, 59 and 76 yards.

"I remember how the ball would just land in my hands," Ismail said. "It was awesome."

Ismail was finally a quarterback's security blanket and was rewarded with a four-year, $8 million contract, a significant raise from $400,000 the previous year.

He began the 2000 season with 102 yards receiving in the season opener before injuring his knee in the second game of the season. By the time he got back into the flow of the offense, the Ravens were in the midst of a month-long touchdown drought and Banks was on the hot seat.

Ismail understood the reasoning behind Banks getting replaced by Dilfer at midseason, but he wasn't happy about it.

"Trent can't throw a lick," Ismail said. "He throws a hard, awkward ball. I'm like, wait a minute, Trent has been throwing to these other guys in practice who have better hands than me and they are dropping them. How in the hell am I supposed to be the go-to guy when he's throwing these awful balls? I'm thinking, *this sucks.*"

It got so bad that, by Ismail's recollection, Billick ordered running plays for an entire red-zone drill in practice because receivers couldn't catch Dilfer's passes.

"I was like, there goes the end of my career," Ismail said. "It was so painful to have that happen."

Ismail, a 1,000-yard receiver with Banks the previous year, failed to produce half that number in 12 games with Dilfer.

He didn't have a catch in the second-to-last game of the regular season. Dilfer only threw to Ismail one time because he was being covered by Aeneas Williams, who had intercepted Dilfer earlier in his career.

Before the Super Bowl, Ismail took his warm-up throws from Banks because he didn't want to be thrown off mentally heading into the biggest game of his career. He caught one pass from Dilfer for 44 yards in the triumph over the New York Giants.

"If we had the ultimate Raven quarterback, it would be the competitiveness of a Stoney Case, the arm talent of a Tony Banks, and the game moxie and intangibles—pull a rabbit out of your butt when everything is falling apart—of a Trent Dilfer," Ismail said.

Over a decade later, Ismail was there again for the Ravens' pursuit of another Lombardi Trophy. He was part of the team's radio announcing team when the Ravens celebrated their second Super Bowl win.

"That ride felt so much like the ride in 2000," Ismail said. "Both of those experiences were so much fun. I think I enjoyed this experience more than the one as a player because I could see all of the subplots that made that year [2012] so special."

Sam Adams

The last big addition to the Ravens' record-setting defense in 2000 was a couple of hours away from playing elsewhere that season.

Sam Adams, the athletically gifted but underachieving defensive tackle, was so frustrated with the Ravens' latest contract offer—it was actually less than what he received the previous season—that he had decided to move on from Baltimore, saying, "I think I'll sign with Green Bay."

Adams was sitting the next morning at Baltimore-Washington International Airport and was prepared to board his flight to Green Bay when he received another call from the Ravens. The sides struck a deal, and Adams soon struck fear in NFL offensive lines.

At 6 feet 3 and 330 pounds, Adams had uncommon agility for his size. He was quick enough to chase down opposing quarterbacks and strong enough to stop the best running backs. He combined an amazingly fast first step (he often was flagged incorrectly for offside) with raw power and a nasty disposition.

"He was the key to taking the defense to another level," middle linebacker Ray Lewis said.

The crazy twist about signing Adams was the Ravens only did so out of desperation. The Ravens needed Adams because they had question marks at both starting spots on the interior of the defensive line. Tony Siragusa was threatening to hold out and Larry Webster was suspended for a year shortly before the draft after violating the substance-abuse policy again.

The Ravens were lucky that a defensive lineman with Adams' ability was unsigned days leading up to the draft, and the team can thank his reputation for that. He was known as unreliable in his six seasons with the Seattle Seahawks. He was called out for taking plays off. One NFC general manager referred to Adams as "a dog."

Adams reinvented himself in Baltimore and answered his critics the only place that mattered. On the field.

"I was [angry] because people questioned my character, my heart," Adams said during the 2000 season. "That's something that just burns me up. Every time I put my hand down [in a three-point stance], I remember that."

Adams certainly played with ferociousness. The Ravens, though, knew what buttons to push to get the best out of him.

It's not a coincidence that Adams went to the Pro Bowl in both of his years with the Ravens and made it there once in his other 12 NFL seasons.

"You can't play on this team and not hustle and put out every time. It shows in the tape," defensive end Rob Burnett said. "It is like being an ink spot on a white sheet. You don't want to be that ink spot."

When Adams first arrived, he was one of the biggest ink spots on the team. Defensive coordinator Marvin Lewis put Adams' name and number on every corner of the big white board in his office, a not-so-subtle reminder to push the stubborn defensive tackle. Lewis was all over Adams at training camp practices and made him repeat plays until he raised his game.

"A lot of times free agents look and say, 'Do I really want to work that hard to be a Baltimore Raven?' I think when Sam said yes, that he did want to, he dispelled all those bogus rumors," defensive line coach Rex Ryan said.

It took some time for Adams to fit into a tight-knit defensive line group, and it took some time for the defensive linemen to understand Adams' mood swings.

Siragusa nicknamed Adams "Sybil," a nod to the 1976 film about a woman battling multiple personalities.

First, there is Sam. "He is laid-back and cool," Siragusa said.

Next there is Samette. "He is whining all the time."

Then there is Sampson. "He is all big and bad."

Lastly, there is Samsonian. "You ask him a question and he just stares into space."

When it came to the Super Bowl, the Giants got a large dose of Sampson. Adams hit Kerry Collins so hard in the third quarter that he separated the quarterback's right shoulder.

A year later, the old Sam Adams resurfaced. With the defending Super Bowl champions losing by 17 points in a divisional playoff game in Pittsburgh, Ryan asked Adams to go back onto the field late in the game. He refused.

Adams never played another snap for the Ravens, and he was released two months later.

Brandon Stokley

Wide receiver Brandon Stokley, the unlikely Super Bowl hero, wasn't sure he was even going to make the Ravens in 2000.

Before the final preseason game that year, coach Brian Billick called Stokley into his office and said: "Listen, just go out and relax. Play football. You're going to make this team."

Then, in the preseason finale, the first pass thrown to Stokley was ...

"Dropped. I dropped it. Unbelievable," Stokley said. "I'm thinking, *if I didn't have one ball thrown to me, I'm making the team. I'm screwing it up now. I'm probably going to get cut now.*"

Fortunately for the Ravens, team officials saw enough potential in the second-year, fourth-round pick to keep him.

Stokley had to bide his time, though. He was inactive for eight of the first nine games of the season and hadn't played since the previous season.

His opportunity came on a November afternoon in Cincinnati, where the Ravens carried a five-game touchdown drought.

That long-awaited score occurred when Stokley turned a soft toss from Trent Dilfer into an electric, 14-yard touchdown pass in the second quarter. The play, called "H Angle Return," was designed specifically for Stokley.

"When Brandon was going to be activated, Brian put that play in for him, because he was killing guys all training camp with that play," wide receiver Qadry Ismail said.

After a fumble recovery gave the Ravens the ball in the Bengals' red zone, the team faced a third-and-eight. Stokley, a role player, was only on the field because it was third down.

He lined up in the slot to the right side, inside wide receiver Jermaine Lewis. While Lewis ran a post pattern, Stokley ran toward the center of the field, then broke out, behind Lewis. Bengals cornerback Rodney Heath bit on the inside move and never recovered.

Stokley took the short pass at the 11 and beat Heath to the corner of the end zone.

"There was a play that we practice and we were looking for a certain coverage. And we got the perfect coverage," Stokley said. "I was barely fast enough to make it to the corner of the end zone over there and dive in there."

It ended the NFL's longest touchdown drought in 26 years and set off pandemonium.

Dilfer danced in front of the Ravens' bench, index fingers shooting flares into the sky. Billick, along the sideline, rammed both arms into the air to acknowledge the elusive touchdown.

And wide receiver Qadry Ismail and guard Edwin Mulitalo lifted Stokley above the gathering crowd in the end zone.

"It was almost like celebrating a playoff win," Stokley said. "That's how it was for the offense anyway. It was good to just get the monkey off our back so you can go out there and play and stop thinking about it and just go play football. It's one of those things where you start kind of thinking about it too much."

The bigger celebration for Stokley and the Ravens happened almost two months later on the grandest stage in football.

On one flashy play, Stokley completely turned the momentum of Super Bowl XXXV by catching a 38-yard touchdown pass from Dilfer just 8:10 into the game.

He charred Jason Sehorn with a quick move and then a bolt down the left sideline. Dilfer put the ball right where it had to be—connecting with Stokley in stride.

For the Giants, it was a stunning development considering that Stokley beat a cornerback with supposed world-class speed and a TV star fiancée.

After Sehorn was dragged into the end zone by Stokley, he got up and glared at teammate, safety Shaun Williams, who bit on a Dilfer look to the left at tight end Shannon Sharpe and was late to help Sehorn.

"I remember looking at the coverage and feeling very comfortable because I'd seen that look in practice a bunch of times," Stokley said. "I thought I might have a chance. Dilfer did a good job of looking off. I didn't expect the guy to blow the coverage. I knew I'd be able to slip

Sehorn inside and give him a good little move and get by him. I just didn't know if we'd get the ball in there quick enough before the guy came over top."

Stokley only caught 60 passes in his first four seasons with the Ravens. After having success with Peyton Manning in Indianapolis and Denver, he returned to play six games in Baltimore in 2013 before suffering a season-ending concussion.

The one play he'll always remember—and be remembered for—was the touchdown catch in the Super Bowl.

"It was definitely a special moment in my career," Stokley said. "It was my second year in the NFL and you never expect to be in the Super Bowl. You couldn't even dream about that, you know. It was so farfetched. To be in that moment and then to catch a touchdown pass, it was just surreal."

Stokley announced his retirement in December 2013, becoming the last member of the Ravens' 2000 Super Bowl team to call it a career.

Sam Gash

Sam Gash came to Baltimore in 2000 with just the shirt on his back. He left with a long sought-after Super Bowl ring.

Gash thought his dreams for a championship were over when he wasn't invited to a training camp that season. He had already lined up a coaching job at Cornell before the Ravens called.

An opportunity unexpectedly came up when starting fullback Chuck Evans went down with a season-ending arm injury in the first preseason game. Gash didn't arrive with any expectations, much less a change of clothes.

"I was going to come down, take a physical, and come back home," Gash said. "Or so I thought."

The Ravens didn't just sign a two-time Pro Bowl fullback. They hired a bodyguard.

For three years, Gash cleared paths for running backs, caused bloody lips, and put would-be tacklers on their backs. Wearing that trademark neck roll, he was a selfless battering ram whose impact was measured by the rushing totals of others.

"I've never seen a fullback give up his body for a tailback like Sam," running back Jamal Lewis said.

It took an injury to open up a spot on the Ravens roster for Gash and it took another one to get him in the starting lineup.

After Obafemi Ayanbadejo suffered a toe injury, Gash started the final nine games in the 2000 season. Not coincidentally, with Gash leading the way, Lewis gained at least 90 yards in seven of them.

"God blessed me to hit people—and I was going to hit them harder than they could hit me," Gash said. "I told our tailbacks, 'Trust me, stay with me and I'll make a hole for you.'"

His last name is fitting considering his physical style on the field.

Besides providing the muscle, Gash delivered "hands-on" instructions at times. After lining up in I-formation, he would flash a certain number of fingers behind his back to his rookie tailback.

"I was giving the snap count," Gash said. It was kind of a reminder to me and a reminder to him. That was the one thing I listened for in the huddle because I knew I had to be quick. I had to know because if I was a step late, it would mess up the play for us. It was kind of like our battle cry like, 'This is the snap count. Now let's go get something done.'"

Not surprisingly, Gash's most memorable play involved a hit. But it wasn't one that sprung open a big run for Lewis.

In the Ravens' first playoff game, Gash was instrumental in Shannon Sharpe's 58-yard touchdown catch and run. After middle linebacker Al Wilson missed a leg tackle of Sharpe, Gash cut off a fast-closing Bill Romanowski with a collision that knocked the Denver outside linebacker several yards out of bounds.

"I was just trying to get anybody close off of him because I knew Shannon had the ability to go," Gash said.

Getting to the Super Bowl was always elusive for Gash. In 1996, he didn't go with the New England Patriots because he was recovering from knee surgery. Three years later, he was on the field when the Buffalo Bills lost an AFC wild-card game as a result of the Music City Miracle.

A career of heartache and a lot of pain—his roughhouse play resulted in 19 orthopedic operations on ankles, wrists, and fingers—made him cherish his 2000 Super Bowl ring even more.

"I wear it to show people something of which I am very, very proud," Gash said. "That season was the culmination of my career."

Chapter 6

MOVING FORWARD

Elvis Grbac

The most debated move in Ravens history resulted in an uprising from the fan base, a vote of no confidence in the locker room, an unexpected retirement, and possibly a tear.

Just over a month removed from hoisting the Lombardi Trophy, the Ravens made the unprecedented decision to not bring back their championship quarterback Trent Dilfer and instead signed Elvis Grbac in what was supposed to be an upgrade.

What is often forgotten is Grbac chose to take on the challenge of quarterbacking the defending Super Bowl champions. A 4,000-yard passer and first-time Pro Bowl player a season earlier, Grbac had other options. Safer and lower-profile options.

He could have re-signed with the Kansas City Chiefs. He could have gone to the Cincinnati Bengals and been closer to family in his hometown of Cleveland. But he signed a five-year, $30 million contract with the Ravens in March 2001, bringing a big arm and even bigger talk to Baltimore.

"It's time that a quarterback comes in here and provides leadership, a go-to guy, a vertical passing game," he said. "This is a great team. I can make it better."

The move was the right one, in theory.

Grbac had better physical tools than Dilfer, not to mention that quarterback look with a 6-foot-5, 240-pound frame. He was groomed in the pro game in the San Francisco 49ers offense, taken to school by Steve Young.

"Let's be honest, he was a better quarterback than Trent," tight end Shannon Sharpe said, "and Brian [Billick] and Ozzie [Newsome] were thinking if he could give us 10 percent more than what Trent gave us, we should be able to repeat."

The harsh criticism of Grbac doesn't always account for the unavoidable problems. Season-ending injuries to running back Jamal Lewis and offensive tackle Leon Searcy in the first week of training camp derailed the offense. Given that, it was impressive that Grbac went 8-6 as a starter and helped the Ravens to the divisional round of the playoffs.

Yet his legacy will be the quarterback who was vilified for making critical mistakes and failing to achieve what Dilfer did the year before—deliver a Super Bowl. Grbac threw a career-worst 18 interceptions, including three returned for touchdowns, and ranked 26th in the NFL in passer rating (71.1).

"We knew coming in, Elvis was going to be held to an unrealistic standard," Billick said. "Anything less than a Super Bowl was not going to be adequate and was going to be his fault. We're a 6-10 team and we're not in the playoffs if it wasn't for Elvis Grbac."

The breaking point for Grbac and his teammates came in the middle of the season when he threw four interceptions, one of which was returned for a touchdown, and lost a fumble in a 27-17 loss to the Cleveland Browns.

Shannon Sharpe was so infuriated that when speaking to reporters after the game, he said, "[Grbac] was brought here to do a job, and the job is not getting done." His comments led Billick to institute a gag order on teammates talking about each other to the media.

It was during that loss to the Browns that television cameras caught what appeared to be a tear running from inside Grbac's eye down his cheek. Ravens officials said it was sweat, and so did Grbac.

"In my heart of hearts, it was a combination of both," wide receiver Qadry Ismail said. "I think he had watery eyes and the sweat made it look even worse. I think he was content on being done, and that was the cathartic moment for him, realizing that he was done."

While Grbac had the superior physical tools to Dilfer, he didn't rally a team like his Super Bowl–winning predecessor had done.

Dilfer was a rah-rah type of a leader whose confidence was infectious; Grbac was a loner whose locker was right next to the exit. Dilfer inspired teammates with emotional rants; Grbac played games with a poker face.

Fans cried out on local radio shows for Grbac to be benched in favor of backup Randall Cunningham. In Grbac's final home game, one man held a sign that read "Elvis, Please Leave The Building."

The 27-10 playoff loss at Pittsburgh summed up Grbac's frustrating season. He threw three interceptions, including one in the end zone that kept the Ravens from cutting into the Steelers' 10-0 lead at that point.

"When a quarterback isn't confident, that makes for a tough day," Steelers linebacker Joey Porter said after the game. "We knew he wasn't going to beat us."

After the season, the Ravens cut Grbac when he refused to take a $5 million pay cut. Three days later, Grbac retired from football because he didn't want to start over with another team and didn't want to move his family again.

"Like I said from the beginning, when I got here, the only mind-set is to win the championship, win the Super Bowl," Grbac said. "And if you come up short, you are a failure."

Todd Heap

Over the years, fans have occasionally approached Todd Heap to sign footballs. He looks down and there it is—a Super Bowl logo.

Winning a championship is the only missing piece from his decorated career. Heap went to Pro Bowls. He set team records. He had thousands of fans screaming "Heeeap" every time he caught a pass.

Sadly, he was drafted three months after the Ravens won their first Super Bowl and was released 18 months before they won their second.

"That's kind of one of those things where unfortunately, I wish I could have been on either one of those teams, but certain things have to do with timing. And timing is everything," Heap said. "I don't ever sit back and stew and fuss. I look back on all the great memories and the fun things and don't really think about that as much."

If there's one Raven who deserves a ring, it's certainly Heap. He took so many hard hits that he doesn't remember how many concussions he's had in his career. He caught a franchise-record 41 touchdowns, 12 more than anyone else in team history, and he accomplished this despite nine starting quarterbacks in 10 seasons.

The Ravens knew the type of receiver and fighter they were getting in 2001. The organization believed its run of good fortune from winning its first Super Bowl was extended when Heap fell to the bottom of the first round.

The consensus top tight end in the draft, Heap was projected to go as high as No. 18. But teams unexpectedly drafted defensive linemen and cornerbacks, allowing Heap to slide to the Ravens at No. 31.

Heap, who was born in Arizona and went to college at Arizona State, was headed to the East Coast for the first time in his life.

"It was funny because I got drafted and I was like, that's about as far away as I could possibly go," Heap said. "But now that I look back at it, those things happen for a reason."

By the time his 10-year career in Baltimore was over, Heap ranked second in team history in receptions (467) and receiving yards (5,492), setting marks that all Ravens tight ends will aspire to beat.

Heap had the smarts to get open and the strong hands to catch everything that came his way. What he lacked was fear. He made his living going across the middle and leaping high in the air in the end zone, putting his body on the line each time.

Of all the touchdowns scored by Heap, his favorite one includes taking a hard shot, of course. In 2006, he scored the winning touchdown with 34 seconds remaining in a 16-13 victory over the San Diego Chargers. After catching the pass from Steve McNair at the four-yard line, Heap collided with Chargers linebacker Shawne Merriman and then dove into the end zone.

It was a surprise to Heap that he even got the ball. He was the third option on the pass play and thought McNair would throw to someone in the end zone considering there was less than a minute left in the game.

"I remember catching the ball thinking, *I'm going to get blown up because it was kind of a higher ball*," Heap said. "Shawne Merriman came over to just try to knock me out, instead of tackle me, and it was the best-case scenario. He kind of bounced off, and I ended up getting in the end zone."

Heap has endured more vicious hits than that one. In 2003, he blacked out after taking a blow to the chin from Broncos linebacker Al Wilson in the end zone. Seven years later, he took a helmet-to-helmet shot from Patriots safety Brandon Meriweather that caused the right side of his body to go numb.

"I did take a lot of hits, but in my mind, some of those hits, I brought on myself," Heap said. "I wasn't catching the ball thinking *go out of bounds or go down*. I rarely had that thought in my mind, if ever. I was thinking, *I'm going catch the ball and I need to get every single yard I can get because I don't know how many times I'm going to touch the ball this week. Or next week.* There are certain situations where I wanted to put the team in the best situation to win."

Putting the team first got Heap into his infamous run-in with Steelers linebacker Joey Porter in 2004. After twisting his ankle, Heap limped to the line of scrimmage so quarterback Kyle Boller could spike the ball and the Ravens didn't have to use a timeout. As Boller thrust the ball downward, Porter shoved Heap backward with a show of brute force.

"When you have that, and my ankle was torn up pretty good, you're just trying to do anything you can do to get the pain to go away,"

Heap said. "I put more pressure driving my head into the ground just to try to get the pain to go to my head, instead of to my ankle."

Years later, Heap confronted Porter about the incident. Porter told him that he was worried that the tight end was faking being injured and was going to run by him to score a touchdown.

Heap didn't buy Porter's story, but he saw a different side of Porter later in his career. When the Ravens released Heap in August 2011, he joined the Arizona Cardinals and became teammates with the former Steeler.

"The funny thing about Joey is when he's on the other team, you absolutely hate him, and I did for many years. I couldn't stand him," Heap said. "But when he's on your team, he's one of those guys you want on your side because you know he's going [to] give you everything he has, and he's going [to] fight to the death for his teammates."

In October 2011, Heap returned to play one more time in Baltimore, although it was in a Cardinals uniform. Two days before the game, Heap took out a full-page ad in *The Baltimore Sun* to thank Ravens fans for the memories.

"My goal was to show my appreciation to the City of Baltimore, the fans, and the organization," Heap said. "I don't even think it does it justice to do that."

Kyle Boller

An obvious hint that the first first-round quarterback in Ravens history wasn't going to make it came two months after Kyle Boller was drafted.

In his first crack at running the Ravens' hurry-up offense at minicamp, Boller had scribbled plays on his left hand, like a kid who was cheating on his first big test.

"I just didn't want to mess it up out there," Boller said.

This is why Boller failed to become the Ravens' franchise quarterback. He was too concerned about making the big mistake instead of focusing on making the big play.

Boller had a big arm, great athleticism, magnetic charisma, and movie-star looks. What he lacked was the mental makeup to play immediately as a rookie.

Rushed into the starting quarterback role for a Super Bowl contender, Boller was so roughed up in his first couple of seasons that it affected how he played the rest of his career.

"Kyle Boller with the Ravens, I love him to death, but you see what getting hit one too many times early in your career can do to you," center Jason Brown said. "He became gun-shy instead of getting the ball and standing back there with poise and then being able to step up. If there was a flash of anything, something—it might have been far to the edge—he was like [flinching]. And he started to scramble. You have to have faith in your offensive line to where you say, 'Hey, I know these guys are going to give me the seconds that I need in order to get this ball off.'"

Boller's bottom line with the Ravens: 42 starts, 45 touchdown passes, 44 interceptions, and no playoff appearances as a starting quarterback.

The combination of Boller's inconsistent play and coach Brian Billick's insistence to start him for three seasons made him one of the greatest hot-button figures in Baltimore sports history.

The fans' level of frustration with Boller turned ugly in the 2005 season opener, when some at M&T Bank Stadium cheered as Boller writhed on the ground in pain with a toe injury.

"I hold no grudge," Boller said. "There will always be people that dislike you. At the same time, there were a lot of people that supported me and I'm very thankful for."

How it unraveled so quickly overshadows the promise that came along with Boller's arrival.

The Ravens' organization made a decision to find a franchise quarterback in the 2003 draft. The team knew it had gotten as far as it could go with retreads and castoffs at quarterback, and Art Modell wanted a star quarterback drafted in his final year as owner to be part of his legacy.

Baltimore had three quarterbacks ranked among its top 10 players, but the Ravens were down to Boller after Carson Palmer was drafted first overall and Byron Leftwich was taken six spots later.

After drafting Terrell Suggs with the No. 10 overall pick, the Ravens traded back into the first round to get Boller at No. 19.

Boller had an arm so strong that he famously threw a ball from midfield through the uprights on one knee during a workout. The most glaring question the Ravens had about Boller was his accuracy, but they decided that had more to do with his teammates.

"Within a couple of years, we learned that Boller's inaccuracy was not solely a result of the poor receivers at Cal, but also Kyle's occasional nervousness in the pocket, which forced his fundamentals to falter at critical times, and has left him a sub-60 percent completion guy thus far in his career," Billick later wrote in his book *More Than a Game*.

"So it didn't work out for Boller, or for me," wrote Billick, who was fired four years after Boller was drafted.

Boller often showed flashes of turning the corner before stumbling because of a lack of poise. The high point for Boller was out-dueling Brett Favre on Monday Night Football in December 2005, when he threw for 253 yards and three touchdowns.

Then there were times when he fumbled without being hit, like the scramble in Cincinnati when he lost the ball two yards from the end zone.

And there was the moment in a 2005 preseason game when Boller missed a handoff to his running back but still tried to make something happen by giving the ball to receiver Derrick Mason on a reverse. Expecting only a fake, a surprised Mason nearly fumbled the exchange before taking a seven-yard loss.

Watching his quarterback compound one mistake upon another, Billick put his right hand on Boller's shoulder and calmly told him, "[Mason] wasn't expecting the ball, so you have to eat that one."

Billick has often said over the years that, if you miss on a quarterback in the first round, you end up doing games on television and not coaching any more.

"If you break it down individually, Kyle had everything you'd want in a quarterback," Billick said. "There were absolutely no negatives. Why that didn't add up, why the whole wasn't as good as the sum of the parts, I don't know. There's no reason he shouldn't have been a good quarterback."

Boller, who finished 20-22 as a starter with the Ravens, expressed no animosity toward the team for replacing him twice during his time here, whether it was trading for Steve McNair in 2006 or drafting Joe Flacco in the first round in 2008.

He remained a consummate professional, never lashing back at fans or pointing fingers at poor pass protection. He repeatedly referred to teammates during his time in Baltimore as "my guys."

"I wish there were more memories and more playoff games and that kind of stuff," Boller said. "But, hey, it is what it is."

After leaving the Ravens in free agency, Boller played three more seasons, bouncing from the St. Louis Rams to the Oakland Raiders. He signed with the San Diego Chargers in 2012 but decided to retire before throwing one pass for them.

Derrick Mason

Of all of Derrick Mason's team-record 471 receptions, the catch that stands out is the most excruciating one.

In the second-to-last game of the 2008 season, when the Ravens were battling for a playoff spot, Mason made a key touchdown grab at Texas Stadium after aggravating a separated shoulder in the first quarter.

"That's the Derrick Mason that we all know and love," coach John Harbaugh said. "Derrick was a guy that you can count on."

Like he did so often in his career, Mason turned around the Cowboys cornerback with an in-and-out move to get open for the 13-yard touchdown. But, this time, Mason ran the route with his shoulder drooping, an injury that forced him to leave the field three times.

Credit: Keith Allison

"I mean, that Dallas game sums him up perfectly," linebacker Jarret Johnson said. "If he is able to move, he's going to be on that field. And if he's on the field, he's going 100 mph. He was trying to fight dudes in that game with one arm."

Before signing Mason in 2005, the Ravens' search for a reliable receiver was futile and frustrating. The Ravens had their trade for Terrell Owens rescinded in 2004 and they couldn't match the Oakland Raiders' trade offer for Randy Moss in 2005. As a result, Baltimore went through the likes of Travis Taylor, Frank Sanders, Devard Darling, Marcus Robinson, Randy Hymes, and Kevin Johnson.

How bad were the Ravens' receivers? The year before Mason arrived, Baltimore's leading receiver was Johnson, who had 35 catches.

Unbeknownst to the Ravens, their future all-time leading receiver had been playing with the hated Tennessee Titans all this time.

"They fell in love with me and I fell in love with them," Mason later said about the Ravens' fans. "Coming from a rival team, that was kind of hard. All that I did on the field, I'm pretty sure I could say the fans could say I gave everything I had. Did I make every play? No, but I made 99 percent of them."

Mason never missed a game during his six seasons with the Ravens and never missed a practice, at least by Harbaugh's recollection. He owns the top three seasons in terms of receptions in franchise history and is the only receiver to catch over 100 passes in a season.

Smart, funny, and articulate, Mason was the vocal and emotional leader of the offense.

"Over the 16 years, 17 years that we have been here, we've signed a lot of free agents, a lot of them. But I don't know if there was any one player over the span of their career that did more for this organization than Derrick Mason did," general manager Ozzie Newsome said. "There could be arguments when you list them all, but what Derrick did in the years that he was here, he would be at the top or near the top and in my mind—at the top because of the number of years that he played here as a guy that wasn't drafted here."

That's high praise for a franchise that signed such free agents as Rod Woodson, Michael McCrary, and Shannon Sharpe.

But Mason was a high-maintenance player. Coach Brian Billick called him "a diva" in his book *More Than a Game*. He even insinuated that Mason was more interested in catches than wins.

According to Billick, Mason was "incensed" in 2006 when the Ravens set a franchise record with 13 wins but he fell short of his usual 90-catch season. A year later, when the team fell to 5-11, Mason caught 103 passes and "acted as happy as a clam."

Mason's preoccupation for catches led to an invitation from Billick to come in on Tuesday after the game plan was set and tell him whether he wanted to line up as the split end, flanker, or in the slot.

"My attempt was to hopefully get him to see that it's kind of hard to orchestrate [catches]," Billick said. "The quarterback's going to go where he's going to go and where the defense dictates it. I don't know if he got it or not but he stopped coming in on Tuesdays."

There was a time in the summer of 2009 when Mason had decided to stop playing football. Mason announced that he was retiring for personal reasons.

It only lasted 20 days. He was back at Ravens training camp, where he pointed out, "T.O. [Terrell Owens] was in Buffalo not even a day and he got a band. I've been here four years and I can't even get the Girl Scouts to come out."

The next day, the Ravens arranged for a local Girl Scout troop to play "Hot Cross Buns" on flutes and recorders. Several boxes of cookies were part of his welcome-back gift.

"I was surprised," Mason said, "but it was a good surprise for me."

Mason's time with the Ravens ended with a few off notes. He instigated a highly publicized sideline squabble with Joe Flacco, which escalated to the point where Mason grabbed the quarterback by the face mask and teammates had to separate the two players. Mason was apparently upset with Flacco for being late on a pass to him. In his final game with the Ravens, an AFC playoff game at Pittsburgh, he was held without a catch for just the second time in his Ravens career.

After being cut by the Ravens, Mason signed with the New York Jets, was traded to the Houston Texans in October, and then released by the Texans in December. But it was important for Mason to retire at Ravens headquarters.

Wearing the same suit he wore when he signed with the Ravens six years earlier, Mason said, "My body left, but my heart stayed right here."

Marshal Yanda

Recounting Marshal Yanda's legendary acts of toughness usually causes the Pro Bowl guard to roll his eyes. The stories either end up being embellished or understated.

In 2007, during Yanda's first training camp, Ravens cornerbacks Chris McAlister and Samari Rolle were fooling around with a stun gun someone had given them. Players threw $600 on the floor and McAlister made an announcement: anyone man enough to voluntarily get shocked with a stun gun can take the money.

"I was a rookie, and $600 was a lot of money," Yanda said. "I said, 'Hell, I'll do it right now.'"

The Ravens should've known better than test an Iowa farm boy. Yanda stepped in the middle of the circle and got zapped. Not once, not twice, but three times.

And he remained standing.

Yanda picked up the cash and delivered a line that provided the biggest jolt of the day:

"That's the easiest 600 bucks I've ever made in my life."

Years later, Yanda believes the dare has been blown out of proportion. Players who weren't there talk about it as if Yanda got hit with a 50,000-volt police-grade Taser.

"That story has been so overhyped," Yanda said. "It was a stun gun, not a Taser. I'm not sure if the batteries were fully charged. I've been shocked by an electric fence on the farm, which is way worse. I used to run into them, get wrapped up, and they'd shock the crap out of you. I got used to them. It was the older fences that would really bite you, where you feel it on the end of your fingertips."

The true testament to Yanda's pain tolerance came toward the end of the 2012 season. He needed emergency surgery on his right leg after a win over the Cleveland Browns on December 24.

A leg whip to his lower leg, close to his calf, caused Yanda to develop compartment syndrome, which is a compression of nerves, blood vessels, and muscle in a section of the body.

Yanda's leg swelled up, and surgeons had to split the muscle to relieve the pressure. A severe case of compartment syndrome can result in loss of a limb, and if not treated, can be fatal.

"It was a nasty scar and a [crappy] way to spend Christmas Eve, but that's what it was," he said.

Yanda was back on the field a week later and made the key block on Ray Rice's first touchdown against the Cincinnati Bengals.

Reporters didn't learn of the surgery until three weeks after it happened. The Ravens had listed Yanda on the injury report with a "thigh contusion," which made him laugh.

Yanda is more than gritty and durable. A third-round pick in 2007, he developed into a three-time Pro Bowl player and one of the best guards in the league.

Before the 2011 season, Yanda signed a five-year, $32 million contract, the second-richest deal ever given to a Ravens offensive lineman, behind All-Pro Jonathan Ogden's contracts.

After agreeing to the deal, he could've flown from his Iowa home to Baltimore or at least hired movers. Instead, he packed a U-Haul full, grabbed his wife and new son, and drove 15 hours through the night.

"Growing up with a farming background, it teaches you to work hard, teaches you to save your money and just to have fun playing the game," Yanda said. "There comes a certain point where you're happy and don't need to change. You've got everything you need."

Grounded and determined, Yanda works hard to show every season that he deserved the contract. In the Ravens' Super Bowl season, Yanda didn't give up a sack and allowed only four quarterback hits.

"There is no one tougher than Marshal," coach John Harbaugh said. "That is a reflection of our whole team. He optimizes that, certainly."

Steve McNair

Steve McNair was traded to the Ravens in 2006, and he brought toughness, a knack for winning, and an air of unpredictability to the quarterback position.

Coach Brian Billick was reminded just how unpredictable McNair could be in his first game after taking over as play caller. It was in New Orleans where Billick watched in disbelief as the Ravens lined up in a formation that he had never seen before and scored a touchdown on a McNair pass.

As the players came off the field, a confused Billick grabbed wide receiver Derrick Mason for an explanation.

Billick: "What formation was that?"

Mason: "Steve didn't call a formation. He just said Toss Right."

Billick: "We don't have a play called Toss Right."

Mason: "Coach, that's all I can tell you. He got us in a huddle and just said, Toss Right. We just lined up and made it work."

Billick went up to McNair and made one request: "Whatever you do, I don't know how you formulated that or how you came up with it, but just do me a favor and tell people that I was kind of involved so they don't think I've lost total control of this offense."

This summed up McNair and how the players adapted to him. He was what Billick called a "game-day guy." He wasn't a quarterback who was going to wow you in the classroom and tell you what route everyone is running. With his experience, he could walk onto the field and just kind of know who would be open. And Billick knew he had to be very precise with the play calls or it would lead to improvisation.

Credit: Keith Allison

The important part was McNair knew how to win. He led the Ravens to a franchise-best 13-3 record and clinched the team's first first-round bye in the playoffs after earning the No. 2 seed.

McNair's influence was evident on the opening drive of the 2006 season, when he marched the Ravens 80 yards on a 14-play, nine-minute drive at Tampa Bay. He then rallied the Ravens from a 19-point deficit against his old team in Tennessee, which was the biggest comeback in Ravens history at that time. In the final month of the season, McNair threw three touchdowns in Pittsburgh just one week after injuring his throwing hand.

"There was no greater warrior or player with a bigger heart than Steve McNair," linebacker Ray Lewis said.

Where it turned bad for the Ravens and McNair's career was in the AFC divisional playoff game against the Indianapolis Colts. In the second quarter, McNair was late on a throw to Todd Heap near the goal line and was intercepted.

The Ravens never got that close to scoring a touchdown again and lost 15-6.

"To end on a shorter note than you intended ... it's very heart-breaking," McNair said after the game. "Do I feel bad? Of course I feel bad. I feel bad that we lost. I feel bad the way I played. There can only be one champion. Unfortunately, this year isn't our year."

McNair was never the same again. He injured his groin early in the 2007 season opener and was limited to six games after developing shoulder and back problems.

On April 17, 2008, McNair walked into a meeting with teammates and shocked them by announcing his retirement at the age of 35.

"It was a hard decision, but I think it's a good decision," McNair said. "I'm always a team player first. Mentally, I could go out there and play. But physically, I just couldn't do it anymore—not to the capacity that I need to help my teammates win a football game."

It was 15 months later when the Ravens had to say goodbye to McNair one final time. In July 2009, McNair was shot dead in his sleep by a 20-year-old girlfriend. He left behind a wife and four sons.

"I've known him for 13 years, and he was the most selfless, happiest, and friendliest person I have known," Mason said. "On the field, there isn't a player that was as tough as him, especially at the quarterback position. What I have seen him play through on the field, and what he dealt with during the week to get ready for a game, I have never known a better teammate."

Chapter 7

NEXT GENERATION ON DEFENSE

Terrell Suggs

Terrell Suggs holds the Ravens' official record in sacks and the unofficial one in laughs. The player affectionately known as "T-Sizzle" is a Pro Bowl talent on the field and an All-Pro clown in the locker room.

Before talking to the media a few days before the AFC Championship Game in January 2009, Suggs wanted the Pittsburgh Steelers to think he was more injured than he actually was. So he started to feign a limp.

There was only one problem. "Sizzle, you have a shoulder injury," a member of the public relations staff told Suggs.

Suggs turned around before any reporters saw him and stepped in front of the microphone with his right arm in a sling. A few days later, he sacked Steelers quarterback Ben Roethlisberger twice.

"You see his personality, and maybe you don't think there is a serious side to him," defensive coordinator Rex Ryan said. "On Sundays, he's all business."

Suggs' personality is a blend of two of the NFL's all-time great passer rushers, combining the humor of Deacon Jones and the trash talking of Lawrence Taylor.

Suggs once wore a T-shirt under his practice jersey at training camp that read, "You Bet Your Sweet Ass I Hate The Steelers!" He once referred to Tom Brady as "God's nephew," and delivered this unforgettable line about Ben Roethlisberger: "His soul may belong to God, but his ass belongs to me."

And when starters proudly named their alma maters during introductions of a prime-time game, Suggs yelled, "Ball So Hard University." It's a line from one of his favorite rap songs.

"I'm a big kid, and I love to have a good time," Suggs said. "I don't think anyone should take themselves too seriously. If you can't laugh at yourself, then who can you laugh at?"

Suggs wreaks havoc on offenses and everyone's ears. He's never quiet. He is constantly screaming at teammates and opposing players during practices and games, often quoting obscure lines from Will Ferrell movies or "The Departed."

His loud-mouth style backfired on him in 2005, when he was ejected from Detroit's Ford Field in the midst of the Ravens setting a franchise-record 21 penalties. He jumped into the face of referee Mike Carey and bumped his face mask against the bill of Carey's cap. Carey said after the game that Suggs "bumped me with malice in his heart."

A somewhat confused Suggs said: "I heard that word [malice] means he felt like I was going to do something. You can't throw somebody out because you think they're going to do something to you. First of all, if I was going to do something to you, I would have done it in the first three steps."

Putting his antics and emotional play aside, Suggs is one of the top all-around linebackers in the league. He's a tenacious pass rusher who can overwhelm blockers with his power or speed. He's a dominant run stopper who has the strength to set the edge. And he's athletic enough to drop back into coverage when he's not chasing down quarterbacks.

His impact all over the field was why he was named NFL Defensive Player of the Year in 2011. Suggs was the only NFL player that season to finish with at least five sacks, five passes defensed, and five forced fumbles.

"If I was going to create a player on the 'Madden' football game, I'd create somebody just like Terrell Suggs to play on my defense," Cincinnati Bengals offensive lineman Andrew Whitworth said. "Physically, he is the biggest, fastest, strongest, and most athletic guy you're going to face in this league. He's everything you'd want in a defensive football player."

If the Ravens had their way in 2003, they would've ended up with quarterback Byron Leftwich and not Suggs.

Baltimore, which had the No. 10 overall pick, had its sights set on Leftwich and coveted the quarterback so much that the team completed a last-minute trade with the Minnesota Vikings to jump three spots to No. 7. But, because the Ravens got a busy signal when trying to inform league headquarters, time expired before they could complete the deal.

Instead, the Jaguars took Leftwich with the No. 7 pick and the Ravens selected Suggs with the 10th. Leftwich has gone on to play for four teams (Jacksonville, Atlanta, Tampa Bay, and Pittsburgh), while Suggs has been to six Pro Bowls in his first 11 seasons.

It was a fateful draft for the Ravens, who never envisioned Suggs on their defense. In the days leading up to that draft, the Ravens ranked their top players and general manager Ozzie Newsome told scouts several times that listing Suggs was "a waste of time" because he was going to be taken in the top five.

Suggs' stock dropped when he ran slow 40-yard dash times in pre-draft workouts. Ravens officials, though, thought Suggs had one of the most explosive first steps they had ever seen.

Ravens coach Brian Billick was asked about Suggs' speed after the team drafted him.

"Well, if the quarterback takes a 40-yard drop," Billick said, "we may be in trouble."

Suggs eventually became the Ravens' all-time sacks leader, surpassing Peter Boulware, and the second-leading tackler in team history behind Ray Lewis.

What can't be measured is Suggs' toughness. In 2012, he tore his Achilles' tendon in late April and amazingly only missed six games. He then suffered a biceps tear and was back after missing two games.

"I'm a guy that doesn't normally doesn't get hurt and had two injuries this year that were supposed to sideline me for the rest of the year," Suggs said, "but I just refused to accept that."

Suggs started to look like his old self in the playoffs, sacking Peyton Manning twice in the divisional round and recording seven tackles in the AFC Championship Game.

Suggs' comeback made him savor his first Super Bowl ring even more.

"Blood diamonds. All that blood for these diamonds," Suggs said. "The journey was long, but it was worth it. It was worth it. But I will tell you this, I damn sure want to feel like this again."

Kelly Gregg

No one has gone from being one of the most hated to most beloved players in Ravens history faster than nose tackle Kelly Gregg.

The first time anyone remembers hearing Gregg's name was August 2001, when he accidentally ended the season for star running back Jamal Lewis. Toward the end of a training camp practice, Gregg did what he was supposed to do and broke through the offensive line to tackle Lewis. But, unfortunately for the Ravens and their Super Bowl title defense, Gregg's hit tore the anterior cruciate ligament in Lewis' left knee.

This wasn't how Gregg, a little-known practice squad player at the time, wanted to gain attention. Gregg thought he was going to get cut the next day.

"Guys were telling me, 'Don't read the Internet, [the fans] hate you!'" Gregg recalled.

Gregg eventually earned the fans' admiration and respect with his blue-collar work ethic and underdog story.

Considered too short and too slow, the Buddha-shaped nose tackle finished his 10-year career in Baltimore with 721 tackles. The only

Ravens player who made more tackles than Gregg over this decade was Ray Lewis.

"He understands leverage better than anybody else," defensive end Trevor Pryce said. "He plays so low to the ground, he can't be moved. And he's stronger than everybody else. He's built like a small VW Bug. Turn a VW Bug sideways and [try to] push it out of the way ... it won't move. That's what he is."

Even though Gregg made first-team All-Big 12 twice at Oklahoma, scouts at the NFL combine looked at his lack of height (six feet tall) and his short arms and mostly rolled their eyes. The Cincinnati Bengals drafted him in the sixth round in 1999, but he never made it off the practice squad. He spent two years with the Philadelphia Eagles and only played in three games.

One day after getting cut by the Eagles, Gregg called Ravens defensive line coach Rex Ryan, his defensive coordinator in college, and made his way down I-95.

What did coach Brian Billick think the first time he saw Gregg?

"Rex, is this guy one of your bastard sons that you're trying to get a job?" he said. "C'mon, you can tell me."

Billick soon nicknamed Gregg "Buddy Lee," the character from the Lee jeans commercials. His easy-going attitude and personality is infectious.

He never complained. In fact, he rarely said much besides "you bet" and "no doubt."

Gregg just rolled up his sleeves and routinely took on multiple blockers in the trenches.

"He might be the best nose tackle in football," linebacker Jarret Johnson said of Gregg in 2009. "Players know that, coaches know that, but the fans, I don't think, really know that."

Opposing teams took notice of Gregg.

"In Denver, anytime we watched film of the Ravens, our D-line coach would go crazy," Pryce said. "He would praise Kelly and say, 'Aaghh, that's the best player in the NFL.' He'd say it all the time. He loved him. Our D-line coach was one of those old hard-nosed guys, and he'd say all the time that Kelly is the best defensive lineman in the NFL."

Gregg was so dominant that he made 13 solo tackles in a game. In 2006, he made 3.5 sacks, which included running down Michael Vick.

"I guess I'd rather be underrated than overrated," Gregg said.

Gregg was cut by the Ravens after the 2010 season for salary-cap reasons, and he played one final season with the Kansas City Chiefs.

Adalius Thomas

Adalius Thomas let people mispronounce his first name for his first three NFL seasons. Not until he made the Pro Bowl in 2003 did Thomas set the record straight on how to say it.

No matter. His friends called him "AD." His teammates referred to him as "The Coordinator." And defensive coordinator Mike Nolan nicknamed him "Defensive Slash."

It was Thomas' uncanny play—not his distinctive first name (which is pronounced ah-DAY-lus, by the way)—that made him unique.

At first glance, Thomas looks like a defensive end. But he hits like a linebacker. He runs like a cornerback. And he thinks like a coach.

The Ravens' unquestioned MVP—Most Versatile Player—not only had the ability to play every defensive position, but he also has already done so. There were games when Thomas went from defensive tackle to defensive end, from outside linebacker to inside linebacker, and from cornerback to safety.

His physical gifts allowed him to play everywhere. His knowledge of the game allowed him to play everywhere remarkably well.

On a defense that boasts all-time greats like Ray Lewis and Ed Reed, Thomas was the first Ravens player to score three defensive touchdowns in a season.

"I've been around football a long time," linebacker Ray Lewis said, "but he's one of those guys, you look back and say, 'Wow.' The thing is, it's not just that AD is one of the most versatile players I've been around. He's also one of the most versatile men I've ever been around."

Thomas came into the NFL as an unknown commodity. In 2000, he was drafted in the sixth round, three spots behind a quarterback named Spergon Wynn.

The knock on Thomas coming out of Southern Mississippi was he took off plays. Others say he just made playing looking too easy.

Thomas spent most of his rookie season, which was also the Ravens' Super Bowl year, on the inactive list. It was far from a wasted year.

"We called him 'The Coordinator,' because he knew everyone's responsibilities," defensive coordinator Rex Ryan said. "He doesn't just know a position, he knows an entire scheme."

It was a matter of pure self-preservation.

"When I was a rookie, if something went wrong, I got blamed for it," Thomas said. "I only knew my job, and I didn't know it very well, so I thought it best to know what everyone around me is doing. It all evolved from there. If you don't know what to do, you can't play fast."

Because of Thomas' thorough understanding of the system, defensive coordinator Rex Ryan woke up one morning with the idea of playing Thomas at safety in some special packages. Ryan proposed the idea to his defensive coaching staff, and no one objected.

There was a game against the Bengals when Thomas lined up across from Pro Bowl wide receiver Chad Johnson.

The loquacious receiver asked, "What's your big ass doing out here?"

It was difficult for anyone to anticipate where Thomas would line up.

He played about 60 to 65 snaps on a top-five NFL defense, where he could be blitzing as a safety or dropping back into coverage as a linebacker. Then, he was on the field for an additional 15 to 20 snaps on special teams, where he had the speed to be a gunner (the player split wide on punt coverage) and the muscle to break up the blocking wedges on kickoff coverage.

"I don't know if there's another player like Adalius Thomas in the National Football League," coach Brian Billick said. "I don't know if there's another player that does all the things that Adalius Thomas does."

Never one to shy away from double duty, Thomas established a charity foundation (appropriately named "Slash") and became a popular figure with the media. Articulate and insightful, Thomas hosted a weekly radio show in the area.

The most popular question posed by fans was: what position does Thomas play?

"I always say I'm just a football player," he said. "Put me on the field, tell me what you want me to do, and I'll do it."

After the 2006 season, the Ravens made the decision to focus their efforts on re-signing Terrell Suggs and let Thomas go elsewhere. Thomas signed a five-year, $35 million contract with the New England Patriots and played three seasons there.

Bart Scott

The hardest hit in Ravens history can be traced back to an apple.

Go back to 2000 when Bart Scott's career was nearly derailed after being suspended the final six games of his junior season at Southern Illinois. It stemmed from an argument during a tense halftime with the defensive coordinator, who told Scott to get rid of the fruit.

When Scott asked why he couldn't eat an apple, the coach slapped it from his hands. Scott pushed the coach, and his season was over.

Scott wasn't asked to the NFL combine. He wasn't invited to college all-star games.

The Ravens were the only NFL team to work out Scott, who was labeled a character risk. Three days after Scott went undrafted, the Ravens brought him in as a rookie free agent. His signing bonus was $500, or $329.60 after taxes.

"I almost had my livelihood taken away over an apple," Scott said. "That's where a lot of my anger [on the field] comes from."

Fast forward to November 26, 2006, when an unblocked Scott leveled Pittsburgh Steelers quarterback Ben Roethlisberger with a hit so violent that it still reverberates with coaches, players, and fans.

This was the day that Scott went from a role player to a feared linebacker.

"That's the cleanest tackle I've had in my life," Scott said. "It felt good to hear the air leave his body."

That most memorable sack was set up with a subtle move.

Instead of blitzing up the middle like he did most of the time, Scott ran to the outside just before the ball was snapped. Steelers running back Willie Parker stepped up to pick up the anticipated pressure, which left Scott free to come off the edge.

"I was 30 yards downfield, and I heard it," Ravens linebacker Terrell Suggs said.

Roethlisberger never saw Scott because he was looking to his left and the linebacker was charging toward him from the right.

"I just kind of remember my head hitting the ground," Roethlisberger said. "He just knocked the wind out of me, and I really couldn't breathe very well, so I just had to lay there a second. That's probably the hardest I've been hit in my life."

Roethlisberger stayed down for several minutes before leaving the game briefly with a bruised chest.

"Those types of hits are forever, you know?" safety Ed Reed said.

Scott believes Roethlisberger was lucky because the hit could've been worse.

"I didn't put the facemask to the sternum," he said. "I left it to the side."

Is there time to make such a decision on the way to crushing a quarterback?

"Oh yeah," Scott said. "You're thinking, *Am I going to try to hurt him, or am I going to hit him hard?* He was exposed, wasn't tensed up because he didn't see me coming. I saw all of his chest, and I could've gone anywhere from the kidneys to the sternum to underneath the chin. I had a 15-yard start. I could have done some serious, serious damage."

Before becoming a starter, Scott was a special teams terror for three years and thought he would inherit the starting job from Ed Hartwell in 2005. Instead, the Ravens replaced Hartwell with free agent Tommy Polley.

It wasn't until Ray Lewis went down with a torn hamstring in October 2005 that Scott got his chance with the first-team defense. If Lewis hadn't gotten hurt, Scott said his future could have been different.

"I would probably be somewhere else trying to make it and wouldn't have the instant credibility," Scott said. "No one would know if I could play a lick."

A trash-talking torpedo, Scott got under the skin of the equally verbose Joey Porter, a linebacker with the Steelers.

"He was like a first-year starter, and I told him, 'I don't argue with nonstarters,'" Porter said.

Scott responded by making nine tackles, and after every one he shouted to Porter on the sideline, "That's one. That's two. That's three. …"

Few could silence Scott during his seven seasons with the Ravens. He left after the 2008 season when he became the first free-agent signing by Rex Ryan for the New York Jets. Ryan wanted Scott so badly that he showed up in his driveway at midnight on the first day of free agency.

Jarret Johnson

Jarret Johnson exacted revenge that every Ravens player and fan has long dreamed out.

Too bad the veteran linebacker can't recall it better.

In September 2008, Johnson paid back Hines Ward for years of alleged cheap shots by hitting the Pittsburgh Steelers wide receiver so hard that he laid him out on his back. Anticipating a shovel pass over the middle, Johnson sniffed out the play and snuffed out Ward.

"When I hit him, I didn't expect him to do a freakin' flip," Johnson said. "I was just kind of reacting to the play. You don't even remember a lot of stuff, and I just remember recognizing the play and kind of sitting back. I don't remember if I took one step or if I ran or what."

Getting recognition for his play didn't happen often for Johnson. He was more than a blue-collar player. He defined the term.

On a defense that was headlined by Ray Lewis and Ed Reed, Johnson handled all of the dirty work—wrestle blockers to set the edge and sacrifice his body.

Johnson wasn't the biggest linebacker and certainly wasn't the fastest. But no one outworked Johnson or gave more effort.

"In 38 years of coaching, he may be the most physical, toughest football player that I've ever been around," former Ravens defensive coordinator Greg Mattison said. "And I can say that [because] ... truly, I and the rest of the coaches will watch tape and we'll say it each time: That's how a Raven plays. Jarret Johnson does it every practice, every snap, every time he is supposed to do it."

During Johnson's seven years as a starter for the Ravens (2005–13), the defense ranked in the top 10 every season. Three other Baltimore linebackers made it to the Pro Bowl in this span (Lewis, Terrell Suggs, and Bart Scott), but the unheralded rock was Johnson.

He played in 130 straight games, a team record. He never missed a game due to injury in his nine years with the Ravens.

Johnson's durability underlines his determination to play through injuries, and not insignificant injuries, either. In 2009, he tore his right labrum in training camp—an injury that would require surgery in the offseason—and then had an AC joint sprain in the left shoulder in Week 2.

But he didn't miss a start, and he became the fourth Ravens linebacker to amass at least 70 tackles, five sacks (he had six), and two interceptions in one season. In 2007, he played with a broken thumb and put up a career-high 94 tackles.

Lewis likened him to a "construction worker" on the Ravens' gritty defense.

"He's just going to always come to work," Lewis said. "He doesn't have that glamorous job ... he just loves doing what he does. And anytime that you can play with a warrior like that, there is no greater reward when you actually get to play alongside somebody like that. His wherewithal—his knowledge of the game and how many adjustments for me and him that we have to make and really talk out—he's just so big a piece for our defense."

Johnson and the Ravens amicably split after the 2011 season. The Ravens wanted to get younger and had Paul Kruger waiting in the wings. Johnson went to the San Diego Chargers in free agency, but not without a parting shot to his longtime rival.

Asked if his departure is less painful because he didn't go to the Steelers, Johnson said, "I told everybody if I went to Pittsburgh, I would've had to throw up on my jersey every time we played."

Haloti Ngata

Haloti Ngata could only stand there on the sideline when the Super Bowl was on the line. With a late goal-line stand against the 49ers, the Ravens' best defensive lineman was a mere spectator because he had injured his knee earlier in the game.

This typified a year of bad luck but ultimately good fortune for Ngata. He battled through the 2012 regular season with a bad right knee and busted right shoulder, a sacrifice that helped the Ravens reach their first Super Bowl in 12 years.

But, in the third quarter, Ngata damaged what had been his one healthy knee on Frank Gore's touchdown run. A 49ers offensive lineman fell into the back of Ngata's leg, causing the hulking defensive tackle to crash to the ground. His knee went numb, and he didn't play another snap in the Super Bowl.

"I definitely wanted to be out there with the guys and wanted to finish off the game," Ngata said. "I'm just happy that they were able to finish it off without me out there."

Ngata has dealt with tougher instances of joy mixed with pain.

Four years after his father was killed in a truck accident, Ngata decided to leave school a year early and declare for the draft to pay the medical bills for his mother, who was suffering from kidney failure. Six days after Ngata announced he was going pro, she died of cardiac arrest while undergoing dialysis.

"We were expecting for her to get out of the hospital that same day," Ngata said. "I talked to her earlier that day and she sounded happy. Then I got the call later that night that she passed."

The Ravens moved up one spot in the draft to make sure they would get Ngata with the No. 12 overall pick. Ngata couldn't hold back tears. There were feelings of accomplishment. There were feelings of loss.

"I was emotional because my parents weren't there," Ngata said. "I was thinking about them a lot. It was a bittersweet moment."

The Ravens had Ngata rated as the fourth-best defensive player in the draft behind defensive end Mario Williams, linebacker A. J. Hawk, and safety Michael Huff. New England Patriots coach Bill Belichick called Ravens general manager Ozzie Newsome that weekend and told the Ravens' general manager that he secured the best player in the draft.

Not everyone had such a high opinion of him. Mark Schlereth, an ESPN analyst and former Denver Broncos offensive lineman, criticized the Ravens immediately after they picked Ngata.

"You're going to need a propane torch to light a fire under this guy," Schlereth said. "I don't see a guy who can control the line of scrimmage. He took plays off consistently. He's on the ground more than the grass. I don't like the pick at all."

For years, Ngata had a clipped article with that quote taped to his bedroom mirror.

"I think people underestimated me," Ngata said.

Ngata has been to five straight Pro Bowls to establish himself as one of the best defensive linemen in the game. He was a major reason why the Ravens ranked in the top five in run defense in his first six seasons in the NFL.

He's so athletic that he has lined up as a fullback in goal-line situations and even ran routes as a receiver. He's so powerful that he broke Ben Roethlisberger's nose when his left hand raked across the face of the Steelers quarterback.

"He might be more than 350 pounds," Steelers center Maurkice Pouncey said. "He hits like he's 500 pounds."

In the Ravens' Super Bowl season, Ngata was the one hurting.

In a year when Ray Lewis and Terrell Suggs were miraculously coming back from injuries, no one talked about the pain Ngata was enduring. Ngata himself didn't talk about it because, as he put it, men in the Tongan culture are supposed to be fearless. Don't cry. Don't show emotion. Don't show that you're hurt.

But those around the Ravens knew what Ngata was enduring. The usually agile Ngata walked gingerly around the locker room. He often leaned against walls to take the pressure off his sprained knee.

The Ravens knew having a beat-up Ngata was better than not having him at all. He lacked explosion and the usual amount of power, but there were times when he flashed glimpses of his old form. In a game against the Redskins, Ngata chased down Robert Griffin III on a scramble 13 yards downfield.

"I mean, that's pretty insane, a 340-pound guy moving that fast," linebacker Paul Kruger said. "No matter how banged up he is, he can still move around pretty good."

Ngata persevered and earned a championship ring—size 15.

"It definitely was tough towards the end of the season," Ngata said. "But you just fight through it, and we got a Super Bowl out of it."

The Harbaugh Era
(2008–Present)

Chapter 8

LEADING THE NEXT CHARGE

Steve Bisciotti

Steve Bisciotti's cousin wouldn't partner with him in 2000 to buy the Ravens because he didn't feel money could be made off of a football team.

So, why did Bisciotti pay $600 million to purchase the team? Because he could ask questions to the head coach and general manager Ozzie Newsome, and they would have to answer them.

"I'm just the Grand Poobah of the Ravens fan club," Bisciotti said.

Like many Ravens fans, Bisciotti grew up rooting for the Baltimore Colts before they left in 1984. A native of Severna Park, Maryland, he remembers going to Baltimore Colts games every year with his family and sitting at the 10-yard line in the lower deck of Memorial Stadium. Bisciotti also went to the Colts' training camp to take pictures with the players. He always asked if he could wear their helmets.

When the Ravens arrived in 1996, Bisciotti was in the stands for their first game, although he wasn't entirely happy. Among the fans who had given a $5,000 deposit in Baltimore's pursuit of an expansion team years earlier, Bisciotti was promised he would get right of first

Credit: Jay Baker

refusal for the best seats. Instead, he sat at the 35-yard line because he hadn't purchased a suite in the new downtown stadium.

"I remember going to my first suite up at the new Oriole Park and thinking, *this sucks up here*," Bisciotti said. "You're so far away from the field. People are talking and barely paying attention to the game."

Getting closer to the game is one reason why Bisciotti was intrigued by owning a sports team. He had the money to do so after building the Allegis Group, a private staffing company he started with his cousin in a cinder-block basement, into a multi-billion-dollar outfit.

In 1998, he was approached about acquiring the Florida Marlins baseball team. He passed. Bisciotti never wanted to own a team just for the sake of making a splash; he wanted to own a team of which he was a fan.

A year later, Bisciotti was approached about buying into the Ravens. Art Modell needed an infusion of cash, and Bisciotti's money allowed the team to add the necessary free agents to help them win the 2000 Super Bowl. Under the terms of the deal, he would own 49 percent of the team for four years before becoming majority owner in 2004.

Bisciotti describes owning the hometown team as "every man's dream."

Taking over the team at the age of 44, Bisciotti was the NFL's third-youngest owner at the time, yet held a reverence for the old guard. He delayed the sale closing, which allowed Modell to attend his final owners' meetings as a full principal owner. When he built the team's new $31 million, 200,000-square-foot training facility, he insisted the most prominent feature in the lobby would be an oil painting of Modell hanging over the stone fireplace.

Bisciotti's fingerprints, however, are all over the franchise. His vision is for leaders to be inclusive and for decisions to be collaborative. He doesn't want a hierarchy, per se. He stresses partnership.

When he voices an opinion, it's considered refreshing or brutally honest, depending on the nature of the conversation. He's up-front and doesn't mince words. No one has to guess what he thinks.

His emotions run as high as anyone's on game days. When it becomes too much, he leaves his seat, walks behind the closed doors, and vents. This is one reason why he doesn't often attend road games anymore. He's regularly seated close to the opposing fans, and he's afraid he'll get into shouting matches with them.

As the owner of the Ravens, Bisciotti wants to be involved, not in charge. He has questions every week for general manager Ozzie Newsome and coach John Harbaugh, but unlike Jerry Jones and Daniel Snyder, he doesn't think he has all of the answers.

"It's my job to challenge," Bisciotti said, "and their job to convince me otherwise."

On Mondays, he watches the previous day's game again and jots down notes. Like many fans, he complains when the Ravens run the ball on first down on six straight series and when receiver Anquan Boldin only had one pass thrown his way in a first half.

On draft day, Bisciotti expresses his opinion, too. In 2002, he wanted to take cornerback Lito Sheppard, and Newsome decided to go with safety Ed Reed. Bisciotti didn't understand why the Ravens would take a safety when cornerback is the more important position.

Newsome's response was that you have to remain true to your draft board.

Sheppard was a two-time Pro Bowl defender in seven seasons with the Philadelphia Eagles, and Reed is considered one of the best safeties in NFL history.

"I kind of learned from that point on that I better not engage too much and try and alter their decision-making," Bisciotti said, "or else we would have had Lito."

Bisciotti's biggest decision came at the end of the 2007 season, when he fired Brian Billick. During what became a dismal 5-11 season, he had given Billick assurances, not promises that he would return as head coach.

What changed? Bisciotti stopped believing the Ravens could win another championship under Billick.

The Ravens went to the playoffs once in Billick's four seasons under Bisciotti. Still, making a coaching change wasn't an easy decision.

"There were two things haunting me," Bisciotti said. "I had just signed him to a four-year deal a year earlier, so I knew I was on the hook for three years. And so, it wasn't the money as much as it would look like I was trigger-happy."

"And the second one was that I knew I would be on SportsCenter. I knew I would take some criticism, and I knew I would be forced into more exposure than I was comfortable with. So when I finally made that decision, those two things I was willing to accept."

Bisciotti immediately set his sights on Dallas Cowboys offensive coordinator Jason Garrett to be the Ravens' next head coach.

"After firing Brian, who had won a Super Bowl, I felt that I could make my mark for Baltimore by being the one to get the hottest assistant," Bisciotti said. "So right off the bat, before I ever met him, my guy was Jason Garrett. I just wanted to deliver the hottest guy because to me, that would be a win in the eyes of Baltimore."

After the first round of interviews, the Ravens began negotiations with Garrett, who had just completed an interview for the Atlanta Falcons head coaching job. Bisciotti went to dinner at his local Mexican joint and was under the impression that his new head coach would be signed by the time he got home at 8 p.m.

It wasn't that easy. The sides were still exchanging counteroffers long into the night. That's when Bisciotti began to get cold feet. He realized that Garrett wasn't deciding between becoming a head coach in Baltimore or Atlanta. Garrett was weighing whether to become the head coach for the Ravens or stay as the offensive coordinator for the Cowboys.

Bisciotti didn't want Garrett in Baltimore if his dream job was in Dallas. At midnight, with the sides about $1 million apart, Bisciotti told Newsome to end negotiations.

"I talked to Jason that night, and I told him, 'If you're that content and interested in staying there, then you're not my guy,'" Bisciotti said. "'So let's just agree to disagree because, if I was losing you to Atlanta, I'd have kept bidding you up. But I'm not bidding you up if you want to stay in Dallas.' It wasn't real pleasant, but it wasn't terrible animosity either. I just thought the stars were aligning, now all of a sudden, this thing has led me completely about-face. It wasn't meant to be."

After calling it off with the biggest-named candidate, Bisciotti ultimately went with the least-known one. John Harbaugh had never been a head coach at any level, and he had never interviewed for an NFL head coaching job.

"Do I like a guy who has to earn his resume?" Bisciotti said. "Absolutely. I've made a living on guys with thin resumes for 25 years, and it's worked out well for me."

Bisciotti's affection for Harbaugh was evident during the 2012 Super Bowl run. In the AFC divisional playoff game in Denver, he thought the Ravens were headed for a heartbreaking playoff loss for a fifth straight year. At home with the flu, Bisciotti sent this text to Harbaugh in the fourth quarter, with the Ravens trailing by a touchdown:

"I've never texted you during a game. We are down 35-28. And I think it's the best game I've ever seen us in the playoffs since 2000. Win or lose I am so proud of the team and proud of you."

Bisciotti said later, "I wanted John to know that I was proud of him. Assuming we lost, what I wanted him to do was go in the locker room, read my text, and put life in perspective, so that he would feel better about himself standing up there having lost another close one. I just wanted him to read that text and just have a peace about himself when he went to the press conference."

The Ravens went on to beat the Broncos and captured the Super Bowl in New Orleans. With a victory cigar in his left hand, Bisciotti shook hands and gave high-fives to players in the locker room.

"It's nice to bring a championship to Baltimore, and as a life-long Baltimore sports fan, I know what it means," he said.

A few months later, Bisciotti revealed at the team's Super Bowl ring ceremony that he had contemplated selling the team after the devastating loss in the AFC Championship Game the previous year.

The playoff losses were weighing on him. He didn't want to end up being an owner in his 70s who was chasing that elusive Super Bowl for 25 years. Bisciotti talked about it with his wife and, for three months, the feeling of moving on from the Ravens was "fairly pervasive."

"I don't have to contemplate it anymore because I gave Baltimore what I set out to do," Bisciotti said, "and now I do sense that pride and I do feel that my legacy will be a good one."

John Harbaugh

John Harbaugh went from being the Ravens' most obscure head coaching candidate in 2008 to landing the job in a span of 18 days. He hadn't been a head coach or coordinator in his career, yet he convinced the Ravens to let him take control of a team that had gone 13-3 only 13 months earlier.

How Harbaugh won the Ravens' trust wasn't as miraculous as some of the plays that followed in the team's championship run. It was nonetheless unexpected and, in the end, the mantra he borrowed from legendary Michigan coach Bo Schembechler—"the team, the team, the team"—trumped any concerns about his inexperience. Harbaugh was the coach that owner Steve Bisciotti wanted from the start, even though he didn't know it when the search began.

Harbaugh's emergence on the Ravens' radar came from someone whose specialty is finding Pro Bowl players, not future Super Bowl–winning coaches.

Eric DeCosta, the Ravens' assistant general manager, was the first to bring up Harbaugh's name when the Ravens' search committee began compiling potential candidates after the firing of Brian Billick. He suggested Harbaugh after receiving several unsolicited phone calls in a 24-hour span from the likes of draft analyst Mike Mayock, TV broadcaster Sean McDonough (the brother of DeCosta's close friend), and someone affiliated with UCLA's coaching search (where Harbaugh finished runner-up to Rick Neuheisel).

It was an outside-the-box recommendation based on the fact that Harbaugh had never interviewed for an NFL head coaching job, let alone been one in his 24 years of coaching. But, as DeCosta points out, some of the best players he's ever drafted were the ones who were under the radar.

"In my experience, there is not really any kind of coincidence when you're evaluating people," DeCosta said. "When I start to hear chatter on any particular player or person, usually there is some amount of credibility to that. When I had all three of them call me, it meant something. I had a conviction about it."

In January 2008, the Ravens' committee had narrowed its initial list of 40 names down to six candidates to be interviewed: Harbaugh; Cowboys assistant head coach Tony Sparano; Colts assistant offensive line coach Jim Caldwell; Jets offensive coordinator Brian Schottenheimer; Ravens defensive coordinator Rex Ryan; and Cowboys offensive coordinator Jason Garrett, who was Bisciotti's top choice.

Bisciotti had never heard of Harbaugh before the search began, and Harbaugh thought his first impression was going to be his last.

In their first private sit-down, Bisciotti asked Harbaugh what percentage of time he spends with players, coaches, and others in the organization, a question Harbaugh hadn't anticipated. Harbaugh threw out some numbers, and Bisciotti told him it was the wrong answer. When Bisciotti excused himself to go to the bathroom, Harbaugh thought he had blown the interview.

Harbaugh later asked Bisciotti for the right answer and took notes as the owner talked about forging relationships and finding the time to get to know everyone in the building. This was integral for the next coach because some team officials believe Bisciotti saw a fractured building and locker room under Billick. The perception was Billick had lost the respect of the defensive players and he "talked down" to others in the organization.

When the committee met again to evaluate Harbaugh at the end of the day, it was clear he wasn't out of the running. In fact, it was the exact opposite.

"We came back and said we think we can get Jason [Garrett], we think he's interested, and yet how about this Harbaugh guy," Bisciotti said. "We all just shook our heads like this guy's a winner. For a dark horse, he was about as impressive as you could have ever hoped, and yet it didn't change my feelings about Jason because he was everything that he was cracked up to be."

When negotiations broke down with Garrett, the Ravens decided to bring back Harbaugh for a second interview, but it wasn't a given that he was going to get the job. This was another test because he was such a reach to be an NFL head coach, and there were questions whether the Ravens could hand over such a talented and veteran team to someone who had been a longtime special teams coach.

After everyone on the search committee met with Harbaugh again, the Ravens' group started picturing him as the coach who could stand in front of a team meeting and on the sidelines at M&T Bank Stadium.

Team officials then brought Harbaugh in front of the entire group to get a few more answers from him. But Bisciotti quickly broke off the line of questioning.

Bisciotti: "You believe you can do this job."

Harbaugh: "I believe with all of the people in this room, I can be a great head coach. I won't be a great head coach because I'm John Harbaugh. I'll be a great head coach because of all of the support and collective intelligence in this room."

Bisciotti: "Well, we want you to be our head coach."

When the Ravens' coaching search began, Bisciotti was asked to detail what he wanted in a leader. Looking back, Bisciotti had described Harbaugh before he even met him.

"What I look for in leaders is a perfect balance of humility and confidence," Bisciotti said. "If you have too much humility, you might not be tough enough for the job. If you show too much confidence, you might be arrogant enough that you don't have enough humility. So to me, I'm looking for a guy that has the right amount of confidence and the right amount of humility. And he just had it in spades."

In his introductory news conference, Harbaugh delivered the vision for what would become an unprecedented run of success.

"There are three important things in putting together a football team: No. 1 is the team, the second-most important thing is the team, and the third-most important thing is the team," Harbaugh told reporters. "We're going to stick with that through and through, beginning to end, and that's what it is all about."

Harbaugh's greatest accomplishment was unifying the team. There was a division between the mouthy defensive players and the underachieving offensive ones. Even in the successful 2006 season, defensive players were calling for the Ravens to run the ball so the offense wouldn't lose games.

In one of his first moves as coach, Harbaugh shook up the locker room. Instead of all of the offensive players in one area, he eliminated the cliques, mixing offensive linemen with defensive ones and putting linebackers next to quarterbacks. There's even a sign that welcomes players into the locker room that reads: "Team, Team, Team."

"When I first stood in front of that team, the rift was palpable, shockingly so," Harbaugh said. "And now the connection is intense. The relationships are so strong, and they continue to need to be built and worked on. But that's what I'm most proud of."

Harbaugh changed the culture as well as the team's consistency. The Ravens, who had been to the playoffs once in the four seasons prior to Harbaugh's arrival, made the postseason in each of his first five

Credit: Keith Allison

seasons. His ability to win—and win at a high level—in a league that prides itself on parity underscores an unprecedented path of success.

No NFL coach won more games (including playoff games) than Harbaugh during his first five seasons (2008–12). No coach in NFL history has won more playoff games than Harbaugh in the first five seasons of a career. He is the only coach to win a playoff game in each of his first five seasons.

His critics contend that he's a good coach with great players. It's true that the Ravens have had at least five players make the Pro Bowl each season under Harbaugh, including six in 2012. What often goes overlooked, though, is Harbaugh's knack for overcoming challenge after challenge. His teams have always survived serious injuries to star players, unpopular divorces with fan favorites, offensive inconsistency, and a near-annual turnover at defensive coordinator (four in his first five seasons).

In 2008, his first season, Harbaugh went with a rookie starting quarterback (Joe Flacco) and guided the Ravens to the AFC Championship Game. In 2011, the Ravens parted ways with the top two receivers in franchise history (Derrick Mason and Todd Heap) before the start of training camp, but Harbaugh got Baltimore to within one failed catch of the Super Bowl. And in 2012, reigning defensive player of the year Terrell Suggs and linebacker Ray Lewis missed a combined 18 games, yet Harbaugh captured another division title and won the Super Bowl.

When you sign up for Harbaugh's program, you're required to follow the rules at practice. Run full speed. Tuck in your shirts. Buckle your chinstrap. And don't ever think of sitting down. If you're not playing the best at that position, Harbaugh won't put you on the field, and it doesn't matter if you're a former Pro Bowl player. Chris McAlister and Bryant McKinnie learned that the hard way.

Harbaugh's tough love isn't for everyone. Bart Scott sounded off on him a few years ago, and Bernard Pollard didn't attend the team's ring ceremony after insinuating there was a problem with Harbaugh.

Harbaugh emphasized that he doesn't hold grudges and has respected every player who has been with the Ravens. In fact, Harbaugh believes one of the biggest factors in being a great coach is building relationships.

"The word I would use is you got to love your players," Harbaugh said, "and I believe Vince Lombardi loved his players. He was tough on them. He pushed them. They probably didn't love him back at the time. But they sure love him now."

Those who've remained have grown with Harbaugh. The Ravens' second Super Bowl team featured just six players (Lewis, Suggs, Ed Reed, Haloti Ngata, Marshal Yanda, and Sam Koch) who were on the team before Harbaugh. For the most part, these were *his* guys.

"It was a lot different his first year," Yanda told *The Baltimore Sun* before the Super Bowl. "He didn't have his guys here, and some guys gave him fits and ticked him off. He didn't have his relationships built. But some of us have been together for five years now and we're more comfortable with him. We've had some great wins and tough losses together. We know him. We trust him, and he knows when it is time to work, we will work."

The moment that resonated the most with players came in October 2012, when the Ravens didn't look much like a Super Bowl team. If not for coach John Harbaugh, the Ravens wouldn't have been much of a team at all.

After getting routed by 30 points in Houston, the Ravens returned from their bye week only to be greeted with the last announcement they wanted to hear. Harbaugh informed the team it would be practicing in full pads.

As grumbles filled the team meeting room, safeties Ed Reed and Bernard Pollard spoke out against Harbaugh's decision. Most coaches, maybe even Harbaugh years ago, would have told the players to sit down, be quiet, and prepare for a physical practice. Instead, Harbaugh wanted to have a discussion. The players talked about how he treated them, and Harbaugh listened.

What could have escalated into an ugly argument essentially became a town hall meeting. And, by the way, the Ravens didn't practice in full pads that day.

"We probably got more accomplished in that half hour toward becoming the champions that we would become," Harbaugh said. "I wasn't too happy when it was going on. It was tough. [But] I couldn't have been happier when we walked out of the meeting."

Three months later, Harbaugh guided the Ravens to the Super Bowl, or as it was called in February 2013, the "HarBowl." The buildup was all about the first time siblings had coached against each other in the championship game. As far as most of the nation was concerned, this was as much about John vs. Jim Harbaugh as the Ravens vs. the 49ers.

Every day for nearly two weeks, the two were asked about each others' careers—John was forthcoming, Jim not so much. Even their parents got in the act with their own news conferences.

When the Ravens held on to beat the 49ers, the brothers met at midfield as the confetti rained down. "I told him I loved him," John said. "He said, 'Congratulations.'"

More than a year later, it remains a touchy subject. John Harbaugh said that Super Bowl is still not talked about with his brother. "It's off limits," Harbaugh said. "We'd probably get into an argument if we did that."

Harbaugh's celebration came with his Ravens family. He shook hands with President Obama during the team's White House visit, and he reminisced at an opulent ring ceremony.

One side of the ring features the wearer's last name and the Ravens' crest, with the words "Play Like A Raven" around it. On the inside of it are the now-famous words from Harbaugh: "The Team, The Team, The Team."

Joe Flacco

Long before winning the Super Bowl in Feburary 2013, the Ravens realized the extent of Joe Cool's calm demeanor at a cold and windy pre-draft workout at the University of Delaware.

Joe Flacco showed up with a bag of footballs and a few of his Delaware receivers. To see how Flacco would react, Ravens officials arrived with brand new NFL balls along with three other collegiate receivers that the team wanted to work out.

Flacco didn't blink. He smiled and asked how they wanted him to start.

The throwing conditions were poor. The footballs were slick. Flacco was unfamiliar with the receivers. And only five of 150 passes hit the ground.

The Ravens wanted to confuse Flacco, and instead, they came away with more clarity about the future of the quarterback position.

Team officials walked to their cars in silence. They didn't even look at each other. With just a month left before the draft, the Ravens didn't want to give anyone watching a hint that they were so impressed with Flacco.

"It was there that we all looked at each other and kind of said the same thing: 'Do you believe what we just saw?'" said Cam Cameron, the Ravens' offensive coordinator at the time.

So, imagine the Ravens' surprise when owner Steve Bisciotti challenged them to draft a different franchise quarterback—Matt Ryan.

"I told those guys that if they had Matt Ryan listed as the best quarterback in the draft, then I'm willing to give up the whole damn draft for him," Bisciotti said. "I told them there is nothing worse for an owner or for them to be managing a business without a franchise quarterback. I said, 'I don't care what we have to pay for him to trade up. We're getting Matt Ryan.'"

The Ravens, who were drafting No. 8 in 2008, knew they would have to jump six spots to No. 2 (and ahead of the Atlanta Falcons) to get Ryan. Baltimore called the St. Louis Rams, who had the second overall pick, and they wanted two first-round picks (2008 and 2009) along with the Ravens' picks in the second and third rounds.

Team officials convinced Bisciotti the smarter play was to trade back, acquire more picks, and take Flacco. The Ravens had Ryan rated as the No. 3 player in the entire draft and Flacco at No. 15. There wasn't much separation between the quarterbacks in the Ravens' opinion. The team's scouts thought Flacco had a lower floor than Ryan, but he had the higher ceiling.

Credit: Nick Wass

The Ravens dropped from a top-10 pick to near the bottom of the first round, which proved too far down to Bisciotti's liking. He started getting antsy that Flacco wouldn't drop to the Ravens. He didn't want to get stuck with a quarterback like Chad Henne or Brian Brohm, who weren't rated anywhere close to Flacco on the Ravens' board.

Bisciotti wanted the Ravens to trade a third-round pick and move up, but Eric DeCosta, the Ravens' director of player personnel at the time, didn't think the team should do it. DeCosta told Bisciotti that Flacco would be there at No. 26.

Bisciotti then looked across the table at DeCosta and told him, "And what if he isn't? What if somebody takes him? Is it going to be worth an extra third-round pick? We have three of them. So, stop being a pick whore. Let's give up a third, and go back and get him, and be done with this."

The Ravens gave up a pick in the third and sixth rounds to Houston in order to go to No. 18 and take Flacco. At the news conference, general manager Ozzie Newsome essentially delivered the coronation of Flacco, calling him "the guy to lead our football team into the future."

ESPN NFL draft analyst Mel Kiper Jr. questioned the pick, saying Flacco was a second-round talent. The biggest criticism with Flacco was he played in Division I-AA against Towson and New Hampshire instead of national powers like Alabama and Texas.

"I had to go down to the minor leagues of college football to prove who I was," Flacco said. "I'm going to carry that with me for the rest of my life and use it for the best."

Flacco provided a glimpse of the future in his first practice with the Ravens, hitting wide receiver Mark Clayton on target with a pass that soared 50 yards in the air.

Middle linebacker Ray Lewis, who watched 15 quarterbacks start for the Ravens from 1996 to 2007, couldn't hide his excitement. "We've got ourselves a quarterback," Lewis told a team official.

The Ravens, though, wanted to bring Flacco along slowly. The plan was to sit him for his entire rookie season. The hope was for Troy Smith to win the starting job.

But, by the third game of the preseason, Flacco went from third-string to starter after Smith came down with a serious tonsil infection and Kyle Boller suffered a season-ending shoulder injury.

"I didn't want to sit," Flacco said. "If you're going to say I'm your guy, then you should play me. I don't see any benefit of sitting and watching."

Flacco won over fans as quickly as he did the Ravens' organization. In his first career start, he surprisingly scored with his feet instead of his arm, running for a 38-yard touchdown in a 17-10 win over the Cincinnati Bengals at Baltimore's M&T Bank Stadium.

In the first half, fans waved purple placards that read, "Wacko 4 Flacco." In the second half, the crowd chanted, "Let's go Flacco," something no other Ravens starting quarterback before him—from Vinny Testaverde to Troy Smith—had ever inspired.

"I kind of thought I heard it, but I wasn't really sure. I thought, 'Why would they be doing that?'" Flacco said with a laugh. "Hey, if I can keep them on my side like that, it will be a good time."

It had taken the Ravens 13 years, but they finally found a franchise quarterback. That just wasn't enough for everyone.

Flacco isn't a fiery leader like Tom Brady. He's never thrown over 25 touchdowns in a season, much less over 50 like Peyton Manning. And he hasn't passed for over 4,000 yards like Aaron Rodgers or Drew Brees.

He's been called a "choker," an "overrated game manager" and a "fluke," or as one ESPN analyst repeatedly called him, "Joe Fluke-O." What's the best way to describe Flacco? His father says "dull." Flacco married his high school sweetheart, and their typical night involves hanging out in the basement watching reality shows. He doesn't hunt, fish, read books, or collect music. His offensive linemen were so stumped when purchasing a gift for Flacco that they ended up giving him a pinball machine, which would keep him entertained between episodes of "Jersey Shore."

While some view his low-key demeanor as a negative, Flacco argues otherwise. Growing up in Audubon, New Jersey, he wanted to emulate Joe Montana, the definition of calm and cool for NFL quarterbacks. You don't get nervous if you're prepared, Flacco insists. More than that, Flacco believes in himself. That's why he chose to transfer from Pittsburgh, where he wasn't getting on the field, to Delaware. That's why he didn't want to sit during his rookie season.

Players and fans rave about Flacco's cannon arm, but his will is just as strong. The driving motivation for Flacco has never been fame or money. It's what both of those represent—respect—and that's proved elusive despite his incredible success. His nine playoff victories are tied with Tom Brady for the most ever by a quarterback in his first five seasons. His 63 wins, including the regular season and playoffs, are six more than anyone else during that same span.

Still, there was national backlash in April 2012, when a radio station asked Flacco where he thought he ranked among the league's quarterbacks. "I don't think I'm top five," Flacco said, "I think I'm the best."

Critics called this unearned arrogance, but this was Flacco being honest.

"I don't care what the truth is. I don't care what the statistics say," Flacco said before the Super Bowl. "I really believe if you're going to be any good in this league, that's how you have to think about yourself."

In this instance, Flacco did put his (actually, the Ravens') money where his mouth was. A few months after saying he was the best, he turned down a contract offer from the Ravens that would've made him among the five highest-paid quarterbacks in the league. Flacco was heading into the final year of his rookie contract, and Bisciotti was wondering what was holding up the deal.

Bisciotti, who had never involved himself in negotiations before, sat down with Flacco in his office for 40 minutes during training camp. The owner told Flacco that he'd never seen a quarterback more criticized than him and this was Flacco's opportunity to shove a $90 million contract in their faces.

Flacco's response? "My critics don't bother me."

"I remember laughing, thinking this is exactly who he is," Bisciotti said. "But it's true, it doesn't bother him. I said, 'Alright then, go win a Super Bowl and come bang on my desk.'"

In the final month of the 2012 regular season, it looked as if Flacco had made the wrong decision to turn down Bisciotti's offer. In a 34-17 loss to the Denver Broncos, Flacco had an interception returned 98 yards for a touchdown. The lasting image from that embarrassing loss was Flacco lying motionless with his face in the turf after a desperate dive to make the tackle.

The key to Flacco's success has been his determination to pick himself up from his failures. In the AFC wild-card game, he threw two touchdowns in the second half to beat the Indianapolis Colts. The next week, he passed for three touchdowns, including the 70-yard Mile High Miracle, to outlast the Denver Broncos.

The playoffs have become Flacco's time, and the critical moment of his career came at the AFC Championship Game. Trailing 13-7 at halftime, coach John Harbaugh made the decision to loosen the reins on Flacco and the offense. Spread out the defense with three receivers. Go no huddle. Put the ball in Flacco's hands.

"I was definitely disappointed by how we played in the first half," Flacco said. "I was getting ready to say, 'Come on, we have to get going here a little bit.' The good thing was everybody came into the locker room with that same mindset. I didn't have to say anything because it was said before I even got a chance to."

For years, Flacco clashed with former offensive coordinator Cam Cameron about the direction of the offense. Flacco argued you can't win a Super Bowl by playing conservatively. He constantly campaigned to attack more on offense.

On a cold and windy day in New England, he got his chance to do just that. Unfazed by pressure and coverage, Flacco rushed his team to the line, shouted out audibles from the shotgun, and carved up every scheme defensive genius Bill Belichick devised. Baltimore scored 21 unanswered points in the second half on three touchdown passes by Flacco.

The Ravens were headed to the Super Bowl again. This time, it wasn't on the strength of defense. It was because Flacco—the quarterback who referred to himself as the best only months earlier—had outplayed two of the best quarterbacks in NFL history.

"At some point, I definitely thought about the fact that, as a team, we were going to have to beat Tom Brady and Peyton Manning to get to where we wanted to be," Flacco said. "That makes it a little bit cooler."

In the Super Bowl, Flacco threw three touchdowns in the first half. His championship moment came in the fourth quarter, when the Ravens held a 31-29 lead over the 49ers. Facing a third-and-inches, Flacco had three choices at the line of scrimmage: hand off to Rice, audible to an option play (which the Ravens had only run once that season), or switch to a pass to Anquan Boldin. Based on how the 49ers lined up, Flacco knew the run and the option wouldn't convert the first down.

Flacco banged his wrists, a signal that he was going to throw. He completed a back-shoulder pass to Boldin, and the Ravens went on to kick a field goal to extend their lead to 34-29. It was the right call, based on what Flacco saw. But it still was a gutsy one to pass when the Ravens needed inches to convert a first down in the Super Bowl.

Harbaugh said after the game that Flacco has "the guts of a burglar." Offensive coordinator Jim Caldwell believes Flacco is "fearless in terms of taking chances."

One month after it seemed like the season was unraveling in a loss to Denver, Flacco was not only a Super Bowl champion, but also the game's Most Valuable Player. His 11 touchdowns and no interceptions were the best postseason numbers put up by a quarterback since Montana, his childhood idol.

"I tell you what: We don't make it easy," Flacco said. "But that's the way the city of Baltimore is. That's the way we are."

Flacco was in line for a huge payday, but he wouldn't have to bang on Bisciotti's desk, as the owner had suggested before the season. How optimistic was Flacco that the sides would reach a new deal? His biggest splurge happened even before he signed his contract. Flacco bought suits for Todd Heap, Dennis Pitta, and himself on a Las Vegas trip after the Super Bowl. Heap and Pitta were stunned because earlier Flacco was complaining that he couldn't find any $10 gaming tables.

How much did the suits run Flacco? "I'm not going to say," Heap said. "But think of what the most expensive suit in Vegas would cost, and it was more than that."

It became official 26 days after the Super Bowl: Flacco signed a six-year, $120.6 million deal. And, befitting Flacco's down-to-earth style, he learned that the agreement had been reached—which made him the NFL's highest-paid player—while at his uncle's house for family pizza night.

"It wasn't necessarily about the money. It was, at that point, about earning that respect and feeling like I was respected around here," Flacco said. "The fact that they have made me that [record contract offer] definitely makes me feel good about how I played and how they feel about me."

On his way back to his New Jersey home after signing his NFL-record contract, Flacco stopped for a 10-piece McNugget meal, with fries and an unsweetened iced tea for $6.99. Months later, he landed a national commercial with McDonald's.

Ray Rice

It took Eric DeCosta about five plays to realize Ray Rice fit what the Ravens wanted in a running back.

"He had a competitiveness about him that I felt would translate very well to our league," said DeCosta, the team's director of college scouting at the time. "He refused to go down, would disappear and then shoot out of the pile. You could see his passion on tape. I took the tape to [general manager Ozzie Newsome] and he saw the same exact thing."

The Ravens were banking that other teams didn't feel the same way. In retrospect, it's difficult to imagine the Ravens without Rice's dashes to the end zone, his 100-yard rushing games in the playoffs, and, of course, his improbable conversion on fourth-down-and-29 in San Diego.

Coming out of college, Rice was viewed as a workhorse running back who lacked breakaway speed. The Ravens were so sure that the

5-foot-8 Rice would go overlooked that they were willing to gamble after taking quarterback Joe Flacco in the first round.

The 2008 draft unfolded like the Ravens thought. Five running backs were taken before the Ravens' turn in the second round, and Rice

Credit: Duane Burleson

was still on the board. Instead of selecting Rice with the No. 38 overall pick, the Ravens took a risk by trading down in the second round to acquire an additional third-round choice. It paid off: the Ravens were able to take Rice with the No. 55 selection and they added safety Tom Zbikowski with the extra pick.

"Coming out of college, I was told I wasn't fast enough, I wasn't strong enough, I definitely wasn't big enough," Rice said. "That's been the story of my life."

Throughout his Pro Bowl–filled career, Rice has shaken off those labels like another tackler. He has been among the most complete running backs of his generation, ranking regularly at the top of total yards each season.

Rice has been the most consistent offensive weapon in John Harbaugh's run as coach, and the Ravens have frequently relied on him at critical moments.

In 2009, Rice set the tone for the AFC wild-card game in New England when he broke his first carry for an 83-yard touchdown. In a game when Flacco struggled, Rice carried the offense with 159 yards and two touchdowns in the victory.

Two years later, Rice ran for 191 yards and two touchdowns in the regular-season finale at Cincinnati to clinch the Ravens' first division title since 2006.

And, in the Ravens' Super Bowl run, he grinded out 131 yards on 30 carries in an AFC divisional playoff win at Denver.

Above all of these performances is that fateful fourth-down-and-29 play in San Diego during the 2012 season. The magic behind "Hey Diddle Diddle Ray Rice Up The Middle"—this is how Rice rhythmically referenced the play after the game—stems from the unbelievable odds against the running back picking up a first down on such a short pass.

There wasn't much hope for the first-place Ravens at Qualcomm Stadium after struggling for most of the game. Trailing by three points late in the fourth quarter, the Ravens were down to a last-gasp shot after Flacco was sacked on third-and-20. They had to get from their own 37-yard line to the Chargers' 34.

Desperation gave way to determination, thanks to a jolt of adrenaline by Rice. After catching the dump-off pass one yard past the line of scrimmage, Rice initially had a 20-yard cushion in front of him (Chargers defenders dropped deep because the Ravens sent four receivers straight downfield).

As the Chargers converged at their 47, Rice cut to his left to elude two lunging tacklers and run through Marcus Gilchrist's arm tackle. He then received a jarring block from Anquan Boldin on safety Eric Weddle at the San Diego 38 before diving straight through two tacklers for the first down.

The Ravens went on to tie the game in regulation and win it in overtime.

"I don't want to take all that credit," Rice said with a spontaneous belly laugh. "I think it was the turning point in our season."

How improbable was this jaw-dropping play? Over the last 25 years (1987–2012), there has only been one longer non-penalty fourth-down conversion.

"I was surprised," Ravens wide receiver Anquan Boldin said. "Fourth-and-29, we throw a checkdown, but I mean if you're going to throw it to anybody, you would throw it to a Ray Rice, a guy who's able to break tackles, and that's what he did."

Without that victory, the Ravens don't win the division. They don't make the playoffs. And they don't play in the Super Bowl.

"I'm going to tell you the truth right now," Ravens running backs coach Wilbert Montgomery said. "It's fourth-and-29, and you throw a check down play to a running back? Do the math; it's not going to work. A three-yard pass, ... and you're asking Joe, 'What in the heck are you thinking about?'"

Logical thinking dictated the Ravens would attempt to pass deep downfield when facing a fourth-down-and-forever situation. Flacco has one of the strongest arms in the NFL, and the Ravens have two fast wide receivers in Torrey Smith and Jacoby Jones.

So naturally, Flacco throws the shortest pass to the shortest player on the field.

"It was really kind of a Hail Mary situation," Flacco said. "We were running down the field and I was hoping because they were playing so soft, sometimes you can kind of get in behind one of those guys and catch them flat-footed and maybe find a soft spot and rip a ball real quick into somebody. I didn't really see anything like that."

Flacco added, "I don't think it was a good shot, but I thought our best shot was to just kind of give it to Ray. It worked out perfect."

Rice's hard-to-believe play inspired thoughts that the Ravens were a team of destiny, which they ultimately proved to be with their Super Bowl triumph.

"One thing about winning the Super Bowl is that you finally realize that everything was worth it," said Rice, who now sports a Super Bowl tattoo on his left bicep. "We'll forever be champions because we won the Super Bowl."

Anquan Boldin

What made Anquan Boldin the most prolific receiver in Ravens postseason history can't be measured. It can only be admired.

Boldin's success in the biggest games of the year is built on the trust of quarterback Joe Flacco. Never the fastest player, Boldin seemed to be covered on every route. With every throw in Boldin's direction, Flacco had to believe Boldin would fight, out-leap, and do whatever it took to come down with the ball.

The play that defined their connection occurred at a pivotal time in the February 2013 Super Bowl. The Ravens had just watched their 22-point lead in the second half dwindle to 31-29 in the fourth quarter. Some might have flinched in this situation. Not Boldin or Flacco.

On third-and-inches, everyone in the Superdome was expecting a run. Instead, Flacco audibled and threw a back-shoulder pass to Boldin. Fighting off bump-and-run coverage at the line, Boldin made his quarterback's guts look genius by making the grab, despite having cornerback Carlos Rogers draped all over him.

Boldin's 15-yard reception extended the drive and set up Justin Tucker's 38-yard field goal to give the Ravens a much-needed cushion with 4:23 left.

"We felt like it was a big moment," Boldin said. "We felt like it was a situation where we had to convert."

Boldin, who had suffered losses in a previous Super Bowl and AFC Championship Games, played the entire postseason like he wasn't going to be denied a championship.

And, for one brief moment, he actually appeared to be enjoying himself. Boldin sometimes came across as grumpy with his one-word answers, but during the Ravens' Super Bowl run, he was smiling.

He produced 145 yards receiving and a touchdown in the AFC wild-card game against the Indianapolis Colts. He scored two touchdowns in the AFC Championship Game at the New England Patriots. And he delivered 104 yards and a touchdown in the Super Bowl.

Flacco called Boldin "a beast" in the playoffs.

"Without him, we don't win the Super Bowl," Flacco said.

Boldin's impact on the Super Bowl season didn't begin with a catch. It started with a hit.

In late November 2012, he delivered a thunderous block on Chargers safety Eric Weddle, allowing Ray Rice to gain the last extra yards needed on fourth-down-and-29. That represented a turning point in the Ravens season.

Coach John Harbaugh said it was "as physical of a block as you will ever see."

Boldin then caught seven passes for 93 yards as the Ravens clinched the AFC North title for a second straight year and set up a postseason to remember.

Before the AFC wild-card game, Boldin told Flacco that he was going to get 200 yards receiving. But he went into halftime without a catch.

Boldin looked like he was on a mission in the second half, catching all five passes thrown his way for 145 yards, a franchise postseason record. His final catch was an 18-yard touchdown in the fourth quarter that sealed a 24-9 win over the Colts.

"We kind of wanted to hold some things back until the second half," Boldin said.

This was a sign of what was to come in the AFC Championship Game. With the Ravens holding a one-point lead early in the fourth quarter, Flacco's three-yard pass in the end zone was so high that only Boldin or LeBron James was going to come down with it. Boldin pulled it in for the touchdown despite two Patriots defenders converging on him.

Boldin's second touchdown of the fourth quarter was another catch where he had to out-jump a Patriots defender in the end zone. It not only punched the Ravens' ticket to the Super Bowl, but it also drew attention from another sport.

Offensive coordinator Jim Caldwell got a text from a friend who is an NBA coach about Boldin's real height.

"In extremely tough situations, he plays big," Caldwell said. "He may be 6-2, but he plays like he's 6-6."

Boldin's clutch play continued in the Super Bowl. What was lost in his 100-yard receiving day was the fact that four of his six catches either extended drives on third down or resulted in a touchdown on third down.

"Everything that you do, everything that you work for is to get to this moment, to get to this point," Boldin said after the Super Bowl. "Over my career, this has been what it's all about. The personal accolades don't mean much to me. The money doesn't mean that much. Winning the Super Bowl, this is why I play. This is why I play through injuries. This is why I get up early in the morning to work out. All for this moment right here."

Six days after winning the Super Bowl, Boldin made it clear that he wanted to play out the final year of his contract in Baltimore.

"I won't play in another uniform," Boldin said. "We have a saying: Once a Raven, always a Raven. And I'll always be a Raven."

Just like quarterback Trent Dilfer learned after the Ravens' first Super Bowl victory, the Ravens don't make business decisions based on sentiment.

Ravens officials asked Boldin to take a $2 million pay cut in order to remain with the team. Boldin said he deserved his $6 million salary he was owed as "a matter of principle."

The Ravens traded Boldin to the 49ers, a team that had just lost to Baltimore in the Super Bowl, for a sixth-round pick and freed up $5.5 million in salary-cap room.

Boldin was among the last to know. He was flying to Africa as part of an NFL players' charity trip when the trade was announced. When he got to Senegal, he turned on his cell phone to see 100 text messages from friends and family, asking if the rumors were true and wishing him luck with his new team.

"I really didn't expect to be traded, especially from the conversations that I had with the Ravens before I left for Africa," Boldin said. "I just thought at some point we would try to work things out, one way or another. I don't think they led me on. The only regret I have is not being able to say goodbye the way that I would like to."

Ed Reed

Safety Ed Reed made game-changing plays when Baltimore needed him the most, even up to the final quarter of his 11-year Ravens career.

After delivering a history-making interception early in the Super Bowl, Reed fittingly closed an emotional and unforgettable chapter of his life with two critical moments in the fourth quarter.

Reed's blitz on Colin Kaepernick's blind side pressured the 49ers quarterback into an incompletion on a two-point try, allowing the Ravens to keep a 31-29 lead. Eight minutes later, Reed slid out to provide double coverage on a fourth-down pass that sailed over everyone's head, which essentially sealed the Ravens' triumph.

Reed, who belted out an off-key version of an Eddie Money song during the Ravens' championship run, said the win gave the Ravens "53 tickets to paradise."

"That's 11 years that are just storybook," Reed said. "I'm proud to say that the last game was a Super Bowl in Baltimore."

If winning the first Lombardi Trophy of his magnificent career wasn't sweet enough, Reed added quite an exclamation point by doing it at the Louisiana Superdome, which is practically in the shadow of his boyhood home.

Sadly, not all the memories were happy ones. His younger brother, Brian, who battled mental illness, died two years earlier after jumping into the Mississippi River.

During Super Bowl week, Reed spent much of his time in the hotel room with the television off and looked at the water from the window.

"It's bittersweet because we have been through a lot," Reed said. "Been through a lot as men. Been through a lot as a team."

Reed has a permanent place in team history and will long be remembered as the third-best player to wear a Ravens jersey, behind Ray Lewis and Jonathan Ogden.

It's amazing to think that Reed came close to never playing in Baltimore. In fact, the Ravens didn't target Reed in the 2002 draft. Team officials were hoping linebacker Napoleon Harris would fall to them. The Oakland Raiders took Harris (who ended up playing for four teams in seven seasons) one spot ahead of the Ravens.

Reed wasn't the fastest or the biggest safety coming out of college. That's why he was there in the bottom third of the first round. What scouts forgot to measure was his relentlessness.

Reed was selected by the Ravens with the 24th overall pick in the 2002 draft, and over a decade later, an argument can be made that he's the best ball hawk safety to ever play the game. His lasting imprint on the game is the plays he made all over the field by taking risks, whether by jumping routes or haphazardly lateraling the ball.

No one can argue with his results. Reed is a nine-time Pro Bowl player. He was the 2004 NFL Defensive Player of the Year, the first safety in 20 years to win the award. He led the league in interceptions for three seasons, and he holds the NFL record for most career interception return yards (1,541) and shares the league record for postseason interceptions (nine) after picking off Kaepernick.

Reed has scored 14 touchdowns in his career (including playoffs), having reached the end zone off interceptions eight times, blocked punts three times, fumble returns twice, and a punt return once.

"Can't say I've ever coached against anybody better than Ed Reed in the secondary," Patriots coach Bill Belichick said.

When it comes to taking the ball from one end of the field to the other, no one is better than Reed. In 2004, he set an NFL record by running back an interception 106 yards for a touchdown against the Browns. Four years later, he broke his own record.

This time Reed picked off Eagles backup quarterback Kevin Kolb in the end zone and immediately broke up the sideline. Reed made his first cut back to sidestep Kolb and then pushed running back Brian Westbrook off to the side. He eluded a diving tackle by lineman Todd Herremans, leaving one more Eagle to beat. After faking out tight end Brent Celek at the Philadelphia 20-yard line, Reed jaunted the rest of the way for a 107-yard return.

Reed gets as much respect from the opposition as he does from his own teammates. "I've told him to his face many times, 'You're the greatest safety ever to play the game,'" All-Pro Pittsburgh Steelers safety Troy Polamalu said. "We all learn from each other, but we all learn most from him. Whenever you see him have a one-interception game, it's disappointing. 'What happened to Ed? He only took it to the 1? He must be injured.' I don't think it's athleticism that makes great plays. He's got a football IQ, a really instinctual way of playing the game."

In the playoffs, he has baffled Peyton Manning and gotten into the head of Tom Brady.

In the 2011 AFC Championship, Brady had a telling message on his wristband:

Find 20 on every play.

"He's pretty much ingrained permanently in my mind," Brady said.

There were times when the Ravens could empathize with opposing quarterbacks because Reed gave them an equal amount of headaches.

Reed was a loose cannon, which made him great as well as frustrating. No one knew where Reed would pop up on the field, and that included quarterbacks and teammates alike. Reed trusted his instincts over the defensive game plan at times, which made him dangerous and unpredictable.

And no one knew what Reed would say. In January 2012, Reed called out quarterback Joe Flacco in the week leading up to the AFC Championship Game. Reed described Flacco as "kind of rattled" a day after the AFC divisional playoff win over Houston and said the quarterback didn't have "a hold on the offense."

In June 2012, Reed was the only player who didn't show up for mandatory minicamp. If that wasn't a big-enough slap in the face, Reed never called coach John Harbaugh to explain why he skipped it. Reed tweeted a few weeks later that he was doing yard work, writing, "Tell the bosses I'm comfortable!"

Four months later, Reed was among the dissenting voices when Harbaugh announced the team was going to have a full-contact practice during the bye week.

Reed isn't a bad guy. Not even close. He's a mercurial one. When Reed had the hood of his sweatshirt pulled down, he would talk to you like you were his best friend. When Reed had the hood on his sweatshirt up, everyone knew not to approach him.

"Ed was a Hall of Fame player and was absolutely brilliant," said Brian Billick, who coached Reed for his first six seasons in the NFL. "But any coach or player that thinks he knows what Ed Reed is thinking or what he's going to do is mistaken or lying. He could do things that would make you scratch your head and think, *what were you doing there?* But it was a whole lot more good than bad. He's just a different guy that way."

Reed was an influential leader for the Ravens. While teammates referred to Ray Lewis as "the general," Reed was considered more of a big brother. He invited the defensive backs to his home, where they broke down film and played video games.

"A lot of people see this as Ray Lewis' team and Ray's defense. Everything about the Baltimore Ravens, a lot of it is focused on Ray," Ravens cornerback Domonique Foxworth said in 2011. "And that's the thing about Ed is, he doesn't care. He gives those impassioned speeches that motivate us as a team from time to time. When there is a gripe on the team, or when we need some rest, he'll go upstairs and confront Coach Harbaugh just as much, if not more, than Ray. But that doesn't get reported, and Ed doesn't care. Because he's genuine. It's not about how it looks. It's not about who's going to be [mad] at him. It's not about who is going to love him. It's about what he thinks is best for the team."

Unlike two of the other Ravens greats—Lewis and Ogden—Reed didn't spend his entire career in Baltimore. After winning the Super Bowl, he signed a three-year, $15 million contract with the Houston Texans.

It proved to be a good decision for the Ravens to let him leave. Reed only played seven games with the Texans before getting cut. He finished out the season with the New York Jets.

"Our hope is that the Hall of Fame players we drafted could play their entire careers with us, but we understand why Ed is moving on to the Texans," general manager Ozzie Newsome said. "He's not the first Hall of Famer to move to another team. He is one of the Ravens' and NFL's all-time greats. Words cannot measure what he did for us, including helping us win a second Super Bowl. We thank him for all he did for Baltimore. Ed will always be a part of the Ravens family."

Chapter 9

DEALING WITH ADVERSITY

O. J. Brigance

The only person to impact the Ravens' championship runs as much off the field as on it is O. J. Brigance.

In January 2001, Brigance set the tone by charging down the field and colliding with a kick returner for the first tackle of the Super Bowl. Twelve years later, he served as the major source of inspiration for the Ravens' second title.

One day while playing racquetball, Brigance knew something was wrong. There was a pain in his right shoulder that didn't allow him to hit the ball with the same velocity. He thought it could be his rotator cuff, but he soon learned that it was far worse.

Brigance is battling Amyotrophic Lateral Sclerosis (ALS), also known as Lou Gehrig's disease. First, he lost the use of his arms. Next, he lost his ability to walk. Then, his ability to talk.

What Brigance never lost was his ability to lead and make others around him better. As the team's senior advisor of player development, he goes to Ravens headquarters three to four times a week.

And he's still alive. Told he had five years to live when diagnosed in May 2007, Brigance is outliving the prognosis with each passing day.

"No one has beaten this thing, but I am going to be the one who does," Brigance told the players in 2007. "They're going to find a cure."

The disease is a progressive and fatal one that shuts down nerve cells responsible for movement. Swallowing becomes difficult. Breathing eventually becomes impossible. But it doesn't impair the brain or any of the senses.

Bound to a wheelchair and unable to use his voice, Brigance writes by using his eyes. He has a DynaVox computer with eye-recognition software that chooses a letter when he blinks at it. His messages are so stirring that coach John Harbaugh has saved every email from Brigance over the past five years.

"O. J., what you've meant to me and everybody around here, you gave us light and no reason to complain or give any excuses," running back Ray Rice said at Brigance's 44th birthday in September 2013. "O. J. has been a blessing to me. Who are we to complain? What he's going through, it kind of brings a sigh of gratefulness."

Brigance was a fighter long before he was afflicted with this disease. In 1996, as an undersized Canadian Football League linebacker, he was rejected by 28 of 30 NFL teams when he called for a tryout, but ultimately had a seven-year career.

After spending four seasons with the Miami Dolphins, where he was voted team captain twice, he joined the Ravens to help them to their first championship. In the Ravens' rout of the New York Giants in the Super Bowl, Brigance had five tackles on special teams.

"O. J. was never one of those guys who was overly talented as a football player," offensive tackle Jonathan Ogden said. "But he was so dedicated and professional about his job. If everybody approached the game like he did, we would have a lot of great players."

After his playing career was over, Brigance was contacted by coach Brian Billick, who offered him a job in player development. He advises players on their future and helps them return to school or finds them internships.

"I think we can all learn something from O. J.," said linebacker Bart Scott, who wore Brigance's No. 57 when he was with the Ravens. "If I can be half the man, player, and husband he is, I think I will accomplish a lot in my life."

Brigance could have chosen to walk away from his job and handle his ordeal privately. A former special teams standout who prided himself on outworking current Ravens in the weight room, Brigance knows he is a shadow of the overachieving player who played on winning teams in the 2001 Super Bowl and the Canadian Football League's 1995 Grey Cup in Baltimore.

"In his heart, he knows he will be the victor," his wife Chanda said.

Brigance has dedicated himself to being a guiding hand to the Ravens' players, preaching to them that adversity makes you stronger.

"I want to let everyone know I'm not afraid," Brigance said. "I've been up against so many challenges, and this is another one. I'm not going to bow down to it."

Cam Cameron

The change that created a prolific Ravens offense for the playoffs was set in motion by a breakdown on defense during the fourth-to-last game of the 2012 regular season.

The Ravens allowed Washington Redskins rookie backup quarterback Kirk Cousins to tie the game with a late two-point conversion, which eventually led to an overtime win for the Redskins. On the bus ride home, coach John Harbaugh made the boldest move of the Super Bowl season by deciding to fire offensive coordinator Cam Cameron.

How are those events related? Harbaugh later acknowledged that he probably wouldn't have parted ways with Cameron if the Ravens had won the game. As it was, the timing was already odd, not to mention unprecedented.

The Ravens were 9-4. They were in first place in the AFC North. They ranked No. 18 in offense, which was disappointing yet not awful. And the Ravens had just scored 28 points, albeit in a loss at the Redskins.

Harbaugh's decision was based more on philosophy than production. During the week leading up to the Washington game, the Ravens talked about throwing the ball to exploit the NFL's third-worst pass defense. But, on Sunday, Cameron put the ball in the hands of

Credit: Keith Allison

his running backs more often than he gave it to Flacco. He called 33 running plays and just 23 passing ones.

Like he had done so many times in his five seasons with the Ravens, Cameron went with gut feelings in the moment, even if that meant veering from a game plan that took six days to prepare.

"What are we doing?" Harbaugh can remember saying to himself during the game. Harbaugh was once again confused by the sudden shift in gears and could only imagine the growing frustration felt by Flacco and the rest of the offensive players.

So, on the short ride back to Baltimore, Harbaugh decided it was time for him to shift gears.

"You're not talking about what's morally right or fair. You're talking about what is best for the team at that time," Harbaugh said. "It usually doesn't take long ... You don't really have to sleep on that. You really pretty much know. And, if you know, you have to make the decision and go do it. Cam is a pro and understood it completely."

Harbaugh handed the offense to quarterbacks coach Jim Caldwell, who had never called a play in the NFL. Caldwell was the anti-Cameron in a lot of ways.

He welcomed suggestions from Flacco and the rest of the players. He sought input from the rest of the coaching staff on how to attack defenses. And, when the game plan was set, it was the same one used on Sunday.

As a result, the Ravens averaged 31 points per game and 410.3 yards in the 2012 playoffs.

"Everybody has a clear understanding of what's expected, how we're trying to attack defenses and what we're trying to do on offense," wide receiver Anquan Boldin said at the Super Bowl. "That's the main thing that [Caldwell] has brought to this offense."

There were rumblings that it wasn't Harbaugh's call to remove Cameron. Asked whether he or owner Steve Bisciotti pushed Harbaugh to fire Cameron, general manager Ozzie Newsome shook his head emphatically before saying no eight times.

Newsome said he spoke to Harbaugh as they both drove home that night after the loss to the Redskins. "I think I might have to make a decision," Harbaugh told Newsome, and he listed the reasons why.

The next morning, Harbaugh approached Newsome with the news.

"When he walked into my office and told me that he was going to make that decision, he had a peace about himself," Newsome said.

Bisciotti insists his only role in the decision was going over the ramifications of it with Harbaugh.

"If you believe that I made John fire him, you have to believe everything else you read about me for the past eight years is a lie," Bisciotti said. "It's as simple as that. I didn't get to where I was by overruling people that have the authority in their contract and with their handshake with me."

What reports also embellished was Harbaugh's relationship with Cameron. They were friends, just not as close as it was often described.

Harbaugh was hired by Cameron to be the special teams coordinator at Indiana in 1997, but it was Jim Harbaugh who had the longer relationship with Cameron from his days playing under him at Michigan.

Still, it was a difficult decision because Harbaugh knew Cameron's family and had attended Bible Study with him over the years. But this was far from a knee-jerk reaction. There was logic behind it, given that Cameron was on a one-year contract.

If Harbaugh had decided in December that Cameron wasn't coming back, why should he wait until after the season to make the move? It made sense that, if Caldwell was going to be the offensive coordinator next season, he should be the one calling the plays for the final three games and the playoffs.

Cameron told the *New York Times* that it was "a brilliant move" because it forced all of the players to become more accountable. If the Ravens had continued to struggle without Cameron calling the plays, the blame would fall more on the players.

Instead, Cameron's firing created a spark that led to a Super Bowl title. The Ravens sent a Super Bowl ring to Cameron, who then gave it to his stepfather.

"Honestly, it meant a lot," Cameron told *The Baltimore Sun.*

Lee Evans

When the Ravens beat the New England Patriots in the AFC Championship Game in January 2013, players left Gillette Stadium knowing they had exorcised their greatest playoff demons. It was only a year before—against the same team, on the same field, and with the same stakes on the line—that a trip to the Super Bowl had slipped through their grasp.

This was a classic tale of redemption for everyone, except for the person who needed it the most.

Wide receiver Lee Evans, who carries the blame for the most devastating game in the Ravens' existence, wasn't there for the cathartic victory. There was no second chance. There was no second pass.

Evans lives with the fact that the last time a throw touched his hands, one that would've sent the Ravens to the Super Bowl in 2012, was slapped away in the waning seconds of the AFC Championship Game.

"That year put a lot of things in perspective for me, being around all those guys and seeing the way that organization is and what they believe," Evans told ESPN. "It was a tremendous challenge for me, mentally and physically, and I think I've been able to grow a ton. I wouldn't change that for anything."

Evans has never hidden from the worst moment of his career. In fact, he has embraced the pain.

After the game, Evans stood in front of the cameras and took full responsibility, saying the most disappointing part was letting his teammates down.

Evans continued to live in Baltimore following the loss, even though he played just one season for the Ravens. He even has a picture of the dreaded play, which he received after requesting it from the Ravens' public relations staff.

"I do think about it," Evans says. "I don't think about it in a negative way, though. I wanted it as a constant reminder to keep pushing, to keep going. I look at that picture, and basically I ask myself, 'Do I want another opportunity to do that again?'"

The Ravens traded a fourth-round pick to the Buffalo Bills for Evans in 2012 because rookie Torrey Smith was struggling. Expectations were high for Evans, who had amassed nearly 6,000 receiving yards in seven seasons in Buffalo.

He just wasn't the same receiver, and it was evident early. An ankle injury limited him to four catches in nine games.

But the Ravens tried to get Evans more involved in the playoffs. He caught a 30-yard pass in the divisional round win over the Houston Texans and made a 20-yard reception in New England.

With 22 seconds remaining and the Ravens trailing 23-20, Evans had the 14-yard touchdown pass from Joe Flacco in his hands—for a second. Undrafted rookie Sterling Moore slapped the ball away from Evans in the end zone when it looked like he seemed to relax.

Just 39 days after the drop, the Ravens released Evans, who had never been cut in his NFL career. He signed with Jacksonville the next season, but he didn't last until the end of training camp with the Jaguars, a team desperate for receivers.

Evans cheered for the Ravens in their Super Bowl run, saying a part of him shared in the excitement "after fully understanding what it feels like to be on the losing side."

Billy Cundiff

Life in the NFL couldn't have been any better for Billy Cundiff than the 2010 season. He was a Pro Bowl kicker who set a career mark with field goals made and signed a long-term deal with the Ravens.

A year later, it couldn't have gotten any worse.

Cundiff missed horribly on a 32-yard field goal that would have tied the AFC Championship Game in New England, a kick that will go down as the worst in the Ravens' existence.

There were piles of hate mail wanting Cundiff out of town. There were calls to sports talk shows calling him a choker.

Days after the botched field goal, Cundiff went to dinner with his wife and kids only to see it replayed repeatedly on every TV in the restaurant.

"What's in the past is in the past," Cundiff said. "If you don't win the Super Bowl in this league, what you do really doesn't matter for the most part. You can take your stats and compare it against other people. If you're not helping your team win the big one, everybody is back to the drawing board the next year."

The tragic part of this heartbreaking piece of playoff history is how Cundiff has taken the brunt of the blame. Missing that chip-shot field goal was more than a one-man meltdown.

Cundiff rushed onto the field because the scoreboard read third down when it was actually fourth down. Ravens kicking consultant Randy Brown insinuated that the Patriots were involved in the scoreboard malfunction, an accusation that coach John Harbaugh later dismissed.

With this confusion, Cundiff barely got set up in time before the ball was snapped. Calling a timeout would've allowed Cundiff more time to prepare.

Asked if he thought about using a timeout in that situation, Harbaugh said, "That never occurred to me. I didn't think that. You know, looking back at it now, maybe there was something we could have done. But in the situation, it didn't seem like we were that rushed on the field. [I] thought we were in pretty good shape."

The Ravens fully intended to keep Cundiff the next season. But undrafted rookie Justin Tucker surprisingly won the job by out-performing Cundiff in training camp and preseason games.

After being cut by the Ravens, Cundiff bounced around three teams over the next two seasons before playing the entire 2013 season with the Cleveland Browns.

"Obviously things didn't work out the way I wanted to in the AFC Championship Game," Cundiff said. "There's a lot of things you can learn from that, but also a lot of things you can learn from the road that I've traveled."

Bryant McKinnie

Bryant McKinnie's maddening time with the Ravens included controversies involving weight, money, and reportedly a stripper named Sweet Pea.

How the Ravens were able to get four dominating games out of McKinnie during their Super Bowl run remains one of the greatest mysteries in team history.

The Ravens knew about the offensive tackle's checkered off-the-field incidents from his days in Minnesota. His problems began in Baltimore during the 2012 season, his second year with the Ravens.

McKinnie was held out of the mandatory minicamp because he weighed 358 pounds, 13 pounds over his targeted number. In addition, he missed the first three days of training camp after hurting his back and never called team officials to let them know of his absence.

The drama continued leading up to the season opener. McKinnie tweeted that he was being released after the Ravens approached him to reduce his salary. The sides finally agreed on a $1 million pay cut, but that didn't secure McKinnie's spot in the starting lineup.

McKinnie was benched for the first 16 weeks of the regular season. Before the finale, McKinnie went into coach John Harbaugh's office to express his frustration over a lack of playing time and explain how he could help an offensive line that had allowed 15 sacks in the past five games.

"Coach Harbaugh wanted to see more from me in practice," McKinnie said. "I explained to him that, being on the scout team, I didn't want to wear out guys like Terrell Suggs and had just been getting in their way to give them a look, but he wanted me to show him what I could really do. So I picked it up."

McKinnie came off the bench in the final regular season game in Cincinnati and proved he should be the starting left tackle again. But it didn't really matter because the Ravens needed him anyway after left guard Jah Reid injured his toe.

So, McKinnie made his first start of the season in the Ravens' first playoff game. Michael Oher moved from left to right tackle, and Kelechi Osemele shifted from right tackle to left guard.

It was a winning combination. Quarterback Joe Flacco was sacked just six times in four postseason games, and the difference was McKinnie.

"It just clicked," Osemele said. "I don't know what it is, but it was just a good fit. We really didn't even have to take many reps before we realized how dominant we could be."

McKinnie's extraordinary postseason run began when he rendered Dwight Freeney into a non-factor during the Ravens' wild-card win over the Indianapolis Colts. He neutralized Elvis Dumervil during the divisional round win over the Denver Broncos.

And, in the Super Bowl, he shut out the 49ers' Aldon Smith, who finished second in the NFL in sacks. On Flacco's 56-yard touchdown pass to Jacoby Jones, McKinnie swallowed up Smith, allowing Flacco enough time to wait for Jones to get open behind the secondary.

"This was a great reward," McKinnie said. "I waited for my time and was able to step in there and help the team go to where it wanted to be."

McKinnie's finish earned him another contract with the Ravens, who re-signed him to a two-year, $7 million deal. But all of the good feelings from the championship season were gone when McKinnie reported to training camp overweight and didn't practice.

To make matters worse, McKinnie's birthday celebration on a party bus got out of control. Wide receiver Jacoby Jones was reportedly hurt when he was hit over the head with a champagne bottle by a stripper known as Sweet Pea.

"I'm not very impressed personally with the report," Harbaugh said. "It's not something we want to be known for. We'd like to think it's not something those guys would want to be known for. It's nothing to be proud of, so I'm kind of disappointed in that sense."

There was just as much disappointment on the field. McKinnie struggled mightily in the first month of the season, which forced the Ravens to trade fourth- and fifth-round picks to the Jacksonville Jaguars for offensive tackle Eugene Monroe.

In McKinnie's final game with the Ravens, he got beat by Miami Dolphins rookie Dion Jordan, who disrupted Flacco's passing motion. It resulted in an interception return for a touchdown that tied the game in the fourth quarter.

Two weeks later, the Ravens traded McKinnie to the Dolphins for a conditional late-round pick.

"It's a good move for us," Harbaugh said. "It's a good move for Bryant."

Torrey Smith

When the Ravens drafted wide receiver Torrey Smith in the second round in 2011, there were questions about his ability to catch the ball consistently. There were no such concerns about his character.

Smith was a father figure to his six younger siblings. He helped raise them from the time he was six years old while his mother attended community college by day and juggled two jobs at night.

His family nicknamed him "Microwave King," which described the extent of his culinary skills. Before he was in second grade, Smith changed diapers, did loads of laundry, and dressed three younger brothers.

Maryland's Ralph Friedgen, Smith's college coach, referred to the wide receiver as "the perfect person."

"When you're an athlete, it gets more attention," Smith said. "For every one of me, there are a million other people in my situation. Like with my mom, there are a million of her, a million other women making mistakes, being in relationships they probably shouldn't be in, and there's a kid that has to help his family—make a decision whether to be positive or turn his back and go the wrong way.

Smith added, "There were certain times when other kids would be able to go and have fun doing something, and I had responsibility. But that's something I would not take back."

His personal life and professional one tragically converged on September 23, 2012, when his younger brother was killed in a motorcycle accident.

Smith was notified of his brother's death at the Ravens' hotel after 1 a.m. and, accompanied by a member of the Ravens' security staff, left immediately to be with his family in Northern Virginia. No one on the Ravens knew if Smith was going to come back and play in the Sunday night game against the New England Patriots.

By that afternoon, Smith walked into the Ravens pre-game chapel service.

Encouraged by his mother to return to the Ravens, Smith also felt a commitment to his teammates.

Less than 24 hours after losing his 19-year-old brother, Smith finished with 127 yards and two touchdowns in a come-from-behind win over the Patriots. But this was a game defined more by moments than statistics.

It began with a moment of silence for his brother Tevin and ended with coach John Harbaugh handing the game ball to Smith in the locker room. Smith walked to the middle of the huddle to take the ball and started crying before telling everyone how much they meant to him.

"I have my family, and I have you as my family," Smith told his teammates. "I couldn't have done it without you guys."

After each of his touchdowns, the sellout crowd of 71,269 at M&T Bank Stadium chanted "Torrey, Torrey, Torrey." Smith, though, took a private moment after his first score to kneel in the end zone and say a prayer.

"I can't see a single person in here handling it as well as he did," quarterback Joe Flacco said, "and kind of turning it into a positive thing and making the most out of that situation."

Smith led the Ravens with eight touchdown catches in 2012, but the Ravens' fastest receiver had a personal score to settle in the AFC divisional playoff win in Denver.

After being shut down a month earlier by cornerback Champ Bailey, Smith made the Pro Bowl defender look like he had lost a step with two touchdowns in the first half. It marked the first time a Ravens player had ever caught multiple touchdown passes in a single game in their postseason history.

Smith's first touchdown came in the first quarter, when he ran past Bailey for a 59-yard touchdown. A quarter later, in the final minute before halftime, Smith leapt over Bailey along the sideline for a 32-yard touchdown.

In a game where the wind chill was minus-1 degrees, Smith continually burnt Bailey.

"On the field, I look at him like everybody else. Afterward, it sinks in that it's Champ and he's one of the great players in the league and has shut down a lot of great players. I beat him a few times. He's a great player, but I'm a professional, too."

Smith added, "I probably could have had four touchdowns."

When the Ravens advanced to the Super Bowl, Smith's five brothers and two sisters traveled to New Orleans to watch him play. In a game that focused on the two Harbaugh brothers, Smith's brother Tevin was not far from his thoughts.

"Even when my brother passed, I've always gone out and played my heart out for my family," Smith said. "I think about all my family every game. That's just life, man. I don't get caught up in the emotional roller coaster."

Cary Williams

Cary Williams' path to the Ravens included two colleges, three trips to an NFL practice squad, and countless odd jobs in between.

But finding a football home was nothing compared to the challenges he faced growing up.

Williams' mother was schizophrenic and was often confined to mental institutions. His father, Cary Williams Sr., was forced to take care of his two sons and went much too far with the discipline.

Credit: Thibous

There were bruises and cuts. Williams wondered if he was ever going to find a way out.

His cousin, who is an ordained minister, eventually took in Williams and his younger brother after child services intervened.

Years later, Williams reconciled with his father. And when the Ravens reached the Super Bowl, his father was in attendance.

"At the end of the day you gotta forgive and forget, man," Williams said. "I know I'm not perfect, and I don't expect anybody else to be perfect. After a while, you gotta give people a second chance, man."

Second chances came into play during his football career.

Williams began at Fordham, where he was kicked off the team for constantly complaining about a lack of playing time. He ended up at Washburn, a Division II school in Topeka, Kansas, that's home to the Ichabods.

To make ends meet during the summers, he unloaded trucks for FedEx, worked at Target, and cleaned at a Frito Lay plant. He also worked for DirecTV, which could make him the first to install satellite dishes only to appear on the NFL Sunday Ticket package a few years later.

"It's just resilience," Williams said. "Being a fighter. Never giving up on my dream and never giving up on the opportunity to put my best foot forward regardless if I was a maintenance guy or I was just a guy who cleaned the streets."

Williams performed well enough at Washburn to get drafted in the seventh round by the Tennessee Titans (229th player overall) in 2008, only to find himself in football limbo once again. He went back and forth from the active roster to the practice squad three times before the Ravens signed him in November 2009.

The Ravens needed a cornerback after putting Fabian Washington on injured reserve, and director of pro personnel Vince Newsome had been a fan of Williams' size and speed. The intention was to put him on special teams and see if he could develop into a starter.

"I didn't even know the Ravens were interested in me," Williams told *The Baltimore Sun*. "In Tennessee, I had been off the squad, on the squad, then back off, and for them to come in and give me an opportunity was crazy. The day they called, my phone was off. I went to pick it up and saw I had like 12 missed calls."

After two years on special teams, Williams stepped into a starting role in 2011 and never missed a start for the Ravens over the next two seasons.

Williams' low point came in Week 3 of the 2012 season, when Tom Brady completed nine passes for 157 yards against him. Williams called it the most frustrating game of his professional career.

"Tom Brady played better than me that day," Williams said. "But whenever I get the opportunity, if that opportunity ever arises, I'll definitely show up next time. It's one of those things that's going to stick with me until I get a chance to redeem myself."

That opportunity came four months later, when the Ravens played at New England in the AFC Championship Game. With the Ravens ahead 28-13, Williams picked off Brady in the end zone with 66 seconds remaining to seal the victory and send the Ravens to New Orleans.

"Once I saw the ball in the air, I knew I had an opportunity to catch that and make a play for my teammates," Williams said. "The most emotional part was me and Ray Lewis talking in the end zone. He was talking about how happy he was for me. He said, 'We're going to the Super Bowl now,' so I said, 'I'm ready. Let's go.'"

After winning the Super Bowl, Williams was told by team officials that he wasn't a priority in free agency. He became one of six defensive starters from that Super Bowl team to not return to the Ravens the following season.

"I completely understand," Williams said. "There's no hard feelings. It's not something that you get upset about it. We won a Super Bowl, and now I'm moving on."

Chapter 10

CLUTCH PERFORMERS

Jacoby Jones

The Ravens won the Super Bowl because of the magical plays made by Jacoby Jones, and Jones was only on the Ravens because he helped them win a playoff game the previous season—when he was with the Houston Texans.

In January 2012, Jones' mishandling of a punt set up the Ravens' first touchdown in the Texans' 20-13 loss in an AFC divisional round game.

There were reports of death threats and Texans fans burning Jones' jersey in Houston. His agent was so concerned that he hired someone to follow Jones home that night to make sure he was safe.

"I made a mistake," Jones said. "It's something I've got to grow from. I apologized to my teammates."

The Ravens had been looking at wide receivers who could also be the team's primary returner, but they didn't sign Ted Ginn Jr. or Eddie Royal in free agency. The Texans released Jones after the first wave of free agency was over, and his misfortune became a stroke of luck for the Ravens.

Baltimore signed one of its Super Bowl heroes two weeks before the first offseason workout.

Jones made a splash in his first season in Baltimore, scoring three touchdowns off returns in a five-game span. He became the first player in NFL history to record two kickoff returns for touchdowns of at least 105 yards in a career. Jones did it in one season.

In the playoffs, he went from being the Texans' scapegoat one year to the Ravens' savior the next. With the Ravens trailing in the fourth quarter in Denver, Jones raced behind two Broncos defenders and caught Joe Flacco's long toss that fell out of the Rocky Mountain air.

The 70-yard touchdown, forever known as the Mile High Miracle, stunned a city and tied the game with 31 seconds left in regulation. Perhaps just as amazing is the fact that Jones knew the unlikely play was going to happen as soon as he lined up.

"Right before the snap, I knew we would look there. I saw an opening," Jones said. "When [Broncos cornerback Tony Carter] didn't jam me and I got by him, it was over with."

As soon as Flacco saw Jones race behind the defense, he stepped up and heaved the ball 54 yards in the air. Jones, who described the pass as a pretty spiral punt that landed in his hands, caught the ball at the 20-yard line before outrunning Carter and safety Rahim Moore to the end zone.

He became only the sixth player in NFL history to score a game-tying touchdown in a playoff game with less than a minute left in regulation that eventually led to an overtime win.

"Nobody thought we could win that game," Jones said. "And down late like that, backed up a little bit, we made it happen. It all came together, but we believed. If you don't believe you can do it, you won't."

When the Ravens advanced to the Super Bowl, they immediately felt at home in The Big Easy, compliments of Jones' family. His mother, who lives in the New Orleans area, fixed 150 plates at the team hotel that included Gumbo, rotisserie chicken, seven-cheese baked macaroni, bell-pepper jambalaya, green peas, potato salad, and bread pudding.

Credit: Nick Wass

Running back Ray Rice told Jones after the Super Bowl that it was "Mama's Gumbo that did it for us."

It was more than home cooking that led to the Lombardi Trophy. Once again, Jones served up the big plays for the Ravens.

His first was a 56-yard touchdown late in the second quarter that showed off his moves as much as his speed. After beating the 49ers cornerback on a double move, Jones slowed up for Flacco's underthrown pass, caught it against his chest, and tumbled backward. He immediately got up where he eluded a safety with the most memorable spin move in Super Bowl history before faking out another defender with a stutter step to get to the end zone.

"That was just backyard football," Jones said. "That's just 'catch me if you can,' like playing freeze tag."

That was Jones' only catch in the Super Bowl. It wasn't his only touchdown.

To open the second half, Jones fielded the line-drive kickoff deep in his end zone and surprised many by not taking a knee for a touchback. This time, it was about his speed, not his moves.

Jones sprinted up the middle of the field, where he was briefly touched at the 20-yard line, but he continued through the open lane in full stride and was gone. The spectacular 108-yard kickoff return put the Ravens ahead 28-6 just 11 seconds into the third quarter.

"All year we've been running along the sideline on the return," Jones said. "They did not expect us to run it down the middle. ... That's my favorite return."

Jones set Super Bowl records for most combined yards (290), longest play, longest kickoff return, and longest kickoff return for a touchdown.

"It's always the goal to win the Super Bowl, and by me being able to come home and play, that was like icing on the cake," Jones said. "You can drop the cherry on it, the strawberry, and the sprinkles."

Jones capitalized on his instant celebrity by competing on *Dancing with the Stars,* where he finished third behind country singer Kellie Pickler and Disney star Zendaya.

Jimmy Smith

Jimmy Smith was a disappointment in his first two regular seasons with the Ravens. Some argued that the cornerback was already a bust.

Smith's career got off to a rough start when he suffered a high ankle sprain on the season-opening kickoff of his rookie season. He then underwent sports hernia surgery in the middle of this second season.

In 2011 and 2012, he had more missed games (nine) than starts (five). It's not what the Ravens had expected from the No. 27 overall pick of the 2011 draft.

"You can ask any No. 1 pick. It's an immediate pressure to produce at a level that the public thinks you should be producing," Smith said. "In your head, since I am a first-round draft pick, I have to come into the league and be the most dominant person to play my position. Especially all of the accolades I got coming in, they expected me to be the best, the most supreme corner. It took me a while to progress."

In a strange turn of events, Smith became the corner everyone envisioned when the pressure on him was at the highest. In the final moments of the Super Bowl, the 49ers needed five yards on fourth down to steal the game away from the Ravens.

Smith knew exactly where the ball was going.

"I saw they wanted to get their best receiver on me," Smith said. "I was actually calm."

It was Smith, the Ravens' No. 3 cornerback, against 49ers wide receiver Michael Crabtree, who had twice as many receptions as anyone else on his team.

When San Francisco quarterback Colin Kaepernick noticed the Ravens' safeties near the line of scrimmage, he decided to call an audible.

"I figured it was either going to be a slant or a fade," Smith said. "I saw Kaepernick tap the back of his head, so I'm thinking it's a back shoulder [pass]. I took away inside leverage just so he wouldn't run a slant, then got my hands on him long enough to mess up the timing."

Smith and Crabtree jostled for position. As the ball neared, Smith grabbed him at the waist while Crabtree pushed Smith away by the helmet.

The pass sailed out of Crabtree's reach and out of bounds. San Francisco coach Jim Harbaugh screamed for a holding penalty. When Smith didn't see any flags on the field, he knew it was time to celebrate.

"I'll never forget that play ever. I don't think the Ravens will ever forget that play," Smith said. "I wouldn't say it was the biggest part of the game. But it was one of those nail-biters in the last minute. In my head, I was thinking the whole time, *it's coming down to me right now.* If I didn't make that play, who knows what would be happening?"

This play changed the Super Bowl as well as Smith's career. Not only did he become a full-time starter the next season, but also he was the best defensive back on the Ravens.

"He's so much more sure of what he's doing. He's not afraid to be wrong," quarterback Joe Flacco said of Smith. "He's not second-guessing himself [thinking], *Should I have done this, or should I have done that?* He's just going out there and playing. I think because of that, his ball skills have improved so much. He's reacting to those things so much better because he's not thinking in his head, *What happens if I don't make the play?* He has confidence, he's very sure of himself, and a lot of the basic things that his talent allows him to do ... He's freed up, and those things are just starting to come out."

Smith, though, still hears from 49ers fans accusing him of holding Crabtree in the end zone.

His response: "The only thing I'm holding now is the championship."

Art Jones

NFL players typically own bragging rights in their families. Not Arthur Jones.

One of his brothers is a mixed martial artist champion, and the other is a celebrated first-round pick for the New England Patriots. Arthur Jones was a fifth-round selection who didn't crack the starting lineup until his third year in the league.

"It hasn't been the easiest road," Arthur Jones said.

Jones now has something his brothers both admire—a Super Bowl ring—and he earned it. For proof, all you had to do was look at his swollen knuckle on his right ring finger leading up to the game.

It came from recovering a critical fumble that was forced by safety Bernard Pollard in the 2012 AFC Championship Game. When the ball was jarred loose, Ravens linebacker Dannell Ellerbe initially jumped on it. But a Patriots offensive lineman pulled it away from Ellerbe, who was playing with casts on both of his thumbs.

Under a pile of five players, Jones ended up taking it back. Four plays later, quarterback Joe Flacco found Anquan Boldin for a touchdown to push the Ravens' lead to 28-13.

"I was in there ripping and prying, and my forearms were burning, but I ended up with the ball at the end of the day," Jones said. "It's brutal under there. Guys are down there trying to break your fingers, and pulling them back. And it's a part of the game. It's a physical game, a very physical game."

Jones came up with another fumble in the Super Bowl. Recovering this turnover was more about hustle than being physical.

After missing a tackle on 49ers running back LaMichael James five yards behind the line of scrimmage, he continued to pursue him downfield. James lost the ball when Ravens linebacker Courtney Upshaw poked it away, and Jones jumped on the fumble before three 49ers players standing there could react.

The Ravens converted that turnover into a Joe Flacco touchdown pass to tight end Dennis Pitta.

"He's turned into an excellent defensive lineman in this league, and I think it is because of his work ethic," coach John Harbaugh said.

Jones drew more attention in the second half, when he tripped up 49ers quarterback Colin Kaepernick for a sack. It was the last play before the power went out at the Superdome for 34 minutes.

"My brother sacked the power out of the Super Bowl," tweeted Arthur's younger brother, Chandler, who is a defensive end for the Patriots.

Arthur Jones' sack dance is unique. He rears his head back, squats, and stomps a couple of times as he waves his arms.

"I'm still trying to come up with a name for it," Jones said. "I'm thinking, 'Time To Get Weird.'"

When the Super Bowl ended, all the cameras turned to John and Jim Harbaugh meeting at midfield. Then it was time for the other brothers to take the field.

Jon and Chandler Jones came down from the stands to celebrate with their older brother.

"When he first started, we'd be out there watching like, 'Is he even playing right now?'" said Jon "Bones" Jones, the UFC light heavyweight champion. "It's very clear that he's come into his own. Not only has Arthur managed to be in the game full-time, but he's becoming an impact player. That's amazing to see."

Corey Graham

Corey Graham was a Pro Bowl special teams player for the Chicago Bears, and he wasn't happy.

"I could go out at practice and get six interceptions at corner, but no matter what, in the meeting I was going to be 'Corey Graham: Special Teamer.' That is just how it was," Graham said. "Sometimes you get labeled like that. Sometimes it's hard to get that label off."

When Graham became a free agent in 2012, teams weren't lining up to give him the opportunity to play defense. Even the Ravens weren't initially interested.

The Ravens were targeting special teams player Blake Costanzo, who decided to take Graham's place with the Chicago Bears. Nine days later, Graham ended up in Baltimore.

The selling point was a chance to compete for something more than a role on special teams.

"There wasn't as much to look at [on film] because he hadn't played that many snaps on defense in Chicago," Ravens coach John Harbaugh said. "But the thing that was interesting about Corey is when he did play on defense he played really well, so we felt like he was going to be a contributor on defense."

For half of the 2012 season, Graham was primarily a special teams player for the Ravens and still a very good one. All of Jacoby Jones' returns for touchdowns came with Graham blocking for him on special teams.

Then, his long-awaited break came to play on defense after injuries to Lardarius Webb and Jimmy Smith. When Webb went down with a season-ending knee injury, the Ravens turned to Jimmy Smith. When Smith suffered a sports hernia injury, it was Graham's first chance to start in over two seasons.

In his second start, his first interception of the season set up a field goal, which proved to be the game-winner in the Ravens' 13-10 win over the Pittsburgh Steelers. This was only a glimpse of what was soon to come.

The Ravens upset the Denver Broncos in an epic playoff win because of Graham's timely turnovers, although they were overshadowed by a more dramatic play. The Mile High Miracle, the memorable, last-minute touchdown pass from Joe Flacco to Jacoby Jones, topped the highlights that night, rather than Graham's two interceptions.

Graham picked off Peyton Manning in the first quarter and returned the ball 39 yards to give the Ravens their first lead. Nearly 71 minutes later, toward the end of the first overtime, Graham's interception essentially sent the Ravens to the AFC Championship Game.

Manning threw an ill-advised pass across his body because he saw Brandon Stokley get open. What he didn't expect was Graham to recover so quickly and undercut Stokley for the interception.

Graham gave the ball to the Ravens at the Denver 45-yard line and set up the game-winning field goal. This was a clutch defensive play from someone who had been pigeon-holed as a special teams player.

"I knew from the beginning it was the best decision I ever made in my life," Graham said of coming to the Ravens before reconsidering his choice of words. "Well, one of the best. Probably marrying my wife was the best."

Bernard Pollard

Bernard Pollard's two sworn enemies are the New England Patriots and pants.

Pollard, the not-so-shy, hard-hitting safety, rarely wore clothes in the Ravens' locker room. He'd come out of the shower with no towel. He'd conduct interviews with reporters in the nude.

When Pollard won the Media Good Guy award in 2012, he was presented with a token of appreciation—a pair of boxer shorts.

"Well, the drawers said it all," Pollard said. "I guess it's an honor."

Pollard's true badge of honor was delivering violent, and sometimes illegal, hits. He was never the fastest defender or an asset in pass coverage. But he was fearless and intimidating.

His physical play set the tone for the Ravens defense, and it wasn't just wide receivers and running backs who paid the price. The fines he's incurred from the NFL during his career have reached six figures, yet he still hasn't toned down his game.

Teams are wary about going over the middle when Pollard is lurking in the secondary. Guess you don't want to test a player nicknamed "Bonecrusher."

"It's a car crash every play," Pollard said. "You can't take away the intensity. This is a grown man's game. You're going to feel it. I enjoy this game. I love giving you my best shot."

His best shot came in the AFC Championship Game in New England, although some will say many of his memorable blows have been on Patriots.

Over a career that began in 2006, Pollard has seriously injured the likes of quarterback Tom Brady (knee, 2008), wide receiver Wes Welker (knee, 2010), and tight end Rob Gronkowski (ankle, 2012).

In January 2013, one step away from the Super Bowl, Patriots running back Stevan Ridley became the latest to feel Pollard's wrath. In the fourth quarter, Pollard accelerated to full speed to unleash a huge shoulder hit on the running back. Ridley's body went limp, and the ball fell out of his grasp. The Ravens recovered the fumble and later scored to secure their trip to New Orleans.

"It changed the whole outlook of the game," cornerback Cary Williams said. "It electrified our sideline, and it electrified our defense."

Ravens coach John Harbaugh called Pollard's vicious collision "the turning point of the game."

"It was just a tremendous hit," Harbaugh said. "It was football at its finest. It was Bernard Pollard making a great physical tackle, just as good of a tackle as you're ever going to see in football right there."

The Super Bowl season was one where Pollard dealt with as much pain as he was inflicting. He forced this critical turnover in the playoffs, and led the Ravens in tackles during the regular season, while playing most of the year with six cracked ribs.

Pollard first got hurt in Week 2 at Philadelphia and then aggravated the injury 12 weeks later in Washington. After missing the last three regular-season games, he returned for the playoffs.

No one outside the organization knew the extent of the injury until after the Super Bowl because Pollard didn't want other teams targeting his injury.

"It's tough dealing with pain," Pollard said. "For us as football players, we know we're going to go through it. At the same time, that's the name of the game. Six of them, yep. Hey, it's up to us to go out there and play, and we did."

How did the Ravens reward him for battling like this? The Ravens cut him about a month after the Super Bowl to create $2 million in salary-cap space.

Pollard insinuated that he was released for his outspoken nature, not his performance. He didn't attend the Ravens' visit to the White House and skipped the team's ring ceremony.

"At the end of the day, I know what happened, I know what took place," Pollard said. "I'm sorry, I just don't want to be in the room with certain people."

Pollard signed with the Tennessee Titans and put his termination letter from the Ravens in his locker as motivation.

Justin Tucker

Justin Tucker isn't your typical kicker. Or rookie. Or person, for that matter.

Most rookies hate when it's their turn to do something to entertain the veterans before team meetings at training camp. Tucker, though, volunteered to do it twice.

After impressing everyone with his Christopher Walken impersonation at the start of camp in 2012, Tucker stepped forward to sing opera. If that wasn't original enough, he gave them the option of hearing it in Italian, Russian, or Latin.

Tucker turned the team auditorium into a concert hall, belting out the Italian aria, "O Sole Mio."

"Everybody's jaw hit the ground," linebacker Jameel McClain said.

Tucker attended the University of Texas, but he didn't want to feel like he was going to class all the time. He majored in recording technology and studied under professor Nikita Storojev, a renowned opera singer.

As a child, Tucker dressed up as Cowboys quarterback Troy Aikman for Halloween and had dreamed of playing in the NFL for most of his life. The challenge was convincing others that he belonged in the league. The Ravens were one of a handful of teams that came to scout him on his pro day.

Four kickers were taken in the 2012 draft, and Tucker wasn't among them. The Ravens invited him to rookie minicamp, but they didn't sign him immediately.

It wasn't until May 29, a month after the draft, that Tucker received a contract and it didn't include a signing bonus. He slept on a mattress on his apartment floor for a couple weeks until he bought his first piece of furniture—a rug that he proudly invited teammates over to see.

Ravens coach John Harbaugh, a longtime special teams coach for the Philadelphia Eagles, knew Tucker had a bright future immediately.

"The first time I liked him was the very first kick," Harbaugh said. "Standing behind him, hearing the ball come off his foot, and seeing how straight it tracked, you could tell that he's just a really talented guy."

The Ravens had intended to stick with Billy Cundiff as their kicker, even after he missed a critical kick in the AFC Championship Game. Tucker changed their minds by outkicking Cundiff in training camp and during the preseason. Harbaugh called it a "gut decision" in choosing Tucker, an undrafted kicker, over Cundiff, a Pro Bowl player two years prior.

How did Tucker celebrate making the team? He went to Chipotle. He ate a burrito and drank a soda by himself.

"My entire career was on the line each of those preseason games so the season opener was no different for me," Tucker said. "I always try to stay calm."

What Tucker had to prove was making kicks when it counted in the regular season and in the playoffs. He had never missed a fourth-quarter kick in college, but he had only one game-winner at Texas.

Coincidentally, his first shot at one came in Week 3 of the 2012 season against the Patriots, a team that went to the Super Bowl because the Ravens missed a kick at the end of the game. On this occasion, Tucker lifted the Ravens over the Patriots with a 27-yard field goal as time expired.

Tucker truly exorcised the ghost of Cundiff in the postseason. After the Mile High Miracle tied the AFC divisional playoff game in Denver, Tucker won it by making a 47-yard field goal in double overtime. It came in subzero wind chills, on a chewed-up field and with nearly 77,000 fans howling at him.

"It got real quiet, real quick," Tucker said of the stadium packed with 76,732 fans.

Ravens kicking consultant Randy Brown compared Tucker to Michael Jordan because of his desire to kick in the fourth quarter.

"I never had the option of coming in and acting or feeling like a rookie," Tucker said. "I was never able to ever think like that. If I did, I would be doing everybody in our building a disservice, because when you're a placekicker you're on an island. It doesn't matter if you're a rookie or a 15-year veteran, you have to perform. You don't have that luxury to study behind somebody for an extended amount of time. You're just thrown into the fire and you've got to do well."

A year later, Tucker won a Monday Night Football game in Detroit with a franchise-record 61-yard field goal. He was voted to his first Pro Bowl.

Chapter 11

Unsung Heroes

Dennis Pitta

When tight end Dennis Pitta makes a big play, cameras often pan to outside linebacker Terrell Suggs.

"That's American Express," Suggs shouts. "He's everywhere you want to be."

While the slogan actually belongs to Visa, Suggs makes a good point. Pitta always seems to be there when the Ravens need him the most.

In 2012, Pitta finished second on the team with 61 receptions. His seven touchdowns tied Todd Heap's single-season franchise record.

Pitta was Joe Flacco's trusted red-zone target in the playoffs, catching a touchdown in three of the Ravens' four postseason games. His five-yard touchdown grab in the AFC Championship Game put the Ravens ahead for good in the third quarter. His one-yard touchdown reception in the Super Bowl staked the Ravens to a 14-3 lead early in the second quarter.

"That's what this league is about," Pitta said, "When you get an opportunity, you've got to capitalize."

Opportunities in football weren't given to Pitta. He earned them.

In high school, he was a 185-pound, skinny wide receiver. Most of his college offers came from Ivy League schools, and no one in Division I was giving him a scholarship.

Pitta decided to walk onto BYU's football team and left as the school's all-time leader in catches and receiving yards.

Some draft experts had Pitta going as high as the second round in 2010. Instead, he fell to the fourth round. He was the seventh tight end drafted that year, and he wasn't even the first one taken by the Ravens. Baltimore selected Ed Dickson one round earlier.

It was time again for Pitta to prove himself. He was so unknown that some of his Ravens teammates didn't even know how to pronounce his name (it's PIT-uh).

Pitta finished his rookie season with more concussions (two) than catches (one), as Dickson received more opportunities behind starter Todd Heap.

Pitta's production grew each season, as did his friendship with Flacco. Pitta and Flacco, as well as their wives, frequently go out together, attending Orioles baseball games or just getting pizza.

The players are always among the first to take the field before games. Three hours before kickoff, Pitta can be seen running routes and catching passes from Flacco in what has become their private warm-up routine.

Their friendship was on full display during the Thanksgiving game in 2011. Flacco wanted everyone on the team to have a signature look for the national television game against the 49ers.

Only Pitta went along with Flacco, and the two sported Fu Manchu moustaches. That just happened to be the night when Pitta caught his first NFL touchdown pass.

While they later acknowledged that the funky facial hair was an "ugly" look, it showed a camaraderie that continues to pay dividends.

"We get along great off the field," Flacco said. "I'm sure that has a little bit to do with it in terms of the chemistry that we have on the field, but the bottom line is, he's a good player."

Credit: David Kohl

Flacco's favorite catch that season from Pitta wasn't a touchdown. It didn't even lead to a score. But it may have saved the Ravens in the AFC divisional playoff game in Denver.

In the second possession of overtime, the Ravens were backed up to their three-yard line and faced third-down-and-13. That's when Flacco hit Pitta down the seam for a 24-yard gain.

If not for that catch, the Ravens would have punted out of their end zone and likely would've given the Broncos the ball in Baltimore territory. Instead, Pitta helped change field position.

"We were in a tough spot, and Dennis stepped up," Flacco said. "That's what he's always done for us."

Paul Kruger

By the end of the Ravens' Super Bowl run, it was a legitimate question to ask who was more ticked off: the quarterbacks who were sacked by Paul Kruger or the pass rusher himself?

Accustomed to 30 to 40 plays per game, Kruger primarily stood on the sideline as a spectator in the biggest game of his career. Kruger, the Ravens' sack leader during the 2012 season, said he was only on the field for 17 snaps in New Orleans.

Afterward, Kruger wondered whether the Ravens already knew he was leaving in free agency the next month. It left him with mixed feelings at a time when his team had reached the pinnacle of the sport.

"I don't know if disrespected is the right word," Kruger said. "I'd say more frustrated, just personally, not having to do with anybody else. I'm a competitive guy and I want to be in there on every play and I think anybody who didn't say that would be lying to you. I've had to have a chip on my shoulder since I came into the league."

Playing time was always a touchy subject with Kruger. A second-round pick in 2009, he was inactive for seven of the first eight games as a rookie.

The Ravens didn't think he was big enough to play the run, but they didn't want him to get too big because he needed quickness to get to quarterbacks. It was a vicious circle of moving from defensive end to outside linebacker and then back again. All Kruger had to show for two disappointing seasons was one sack.

Strangely enough, Kruger's best stretch of games for the Ravens were his last ones. He recorded 7.5 sacks in the final eight regular-season games of 2012.

In the Ravens' wild-card victory over Indianapolis, Kruger spent nearly as much time in the Colts' backfield as Andrew Luck. Kruger had 2.5 sacks—the second-most in a playoff game in the Ravens' history—made four tackles, deflected a pass, and caused a fumble.

A week later in Denver, he was responsible for flushing out Peyton Manning in overtime and causing him to throw a reckless pass, which led to Corey Graham's interception and Justin Tucker's game-winning field goal.

In the Super Bowl, Kruger made an impact despite a cameo appearance. He sacked Colin Kaepernick twice, the first time forcing the 49ers to settle for a field goal on their second possession.

So, why wasn't Kruger able to get more playing time with the Ravens?

"I don't know. I tried to figure it out for a while," Kruger said. "It was just one of those things that you got to trust your abilities when you get the opportunity and make the most of every moment. It could be a number of different reasons why, and honestly it's hard to say. There are some answers that you're never going to get. For me, I felt like I should be on the field a lot more. It is what it is."

The next season, Kruger left Baltimore for Cleveland, where he was the Browns' highest-paid free agent that offseason.

"Baltimore was a great experience and an honor to be a part of that team," Kruger said. "I had a great relationship with my coaches and all of my teammates. But the playing time was definitely an issue for me. It's in the past and great things happened there."

Matt Birk

In 2012, there were 49 players on the Ravens' 53-man roster who had never played in a Super Bowl. No one appreciated the trip there more than center Matt Birk.

He reached football's biggest stage after 15 seasons and 227 games played. It's why Birk decided to return for one final season after being bothered by neck, elbow, and knee injuries during his previous three years.

"At that stage in my career, losing takes a lot out of you," Birk said. "I wouldn't have come back if I didn't think there was a legitimate chance that I could help the team. You're just thankful to be on a team that you feel has a chance. With the success we've had around here, it was a Super-Bowl-or-bust mentality."

Before the 2012 season, Birk had been to the playoffs eight times (five with the Vikings and three with the Ravens) and left with heartache instead of a championship ring.

In his first season, Birk watched kicker Gary Anderson miss a 38-yard field goal late in the fourth quarter of the NFC Championship Game that cost the Vikings a trip to the Super Bowl. It was another painful finish for Birk in 2012, when Lee Evans failed to make the winning catch in the end zone in the AFC Championship Game and Billy missed a 32-yarder to tie the game.

"My first year, we were two minutes away from going to the Super Bowl," Birk said. "I thought there was nothing to this. It didn't work out."

Birk was the model of durability for offensive linemen. Despite numerous injuries, including arthroscopic knee surgery just weeks before the 2011 season, he finished his career with 112 consecutive starts, which stood as the NFL's longest active streak among centers.

"Matt's influence in his four years with the Ravens is evident to all," general manager Ozzie Newsome said. "First, he played well and gave us stability on the offensive line. ... Second, his leadership on and off the field was outstanding. We could go to young players and say, 'Do what Matt does and you'll succeed. Watch him and follow him.' His work ethic was as good as any player we had."

Birk never anticipated a career like the one he enjoyed. He went to Harvard and earned a degree in economics. It's easier to name US presidents who graduated from the Ivy League than pro football players.

Nonetheless, Birk was picked in the sixth round by the Minnesota Vikings in 1998.

"I was thinking my [NFL career] would be pretty quick," Birk said. "Not really a career, more of just an experience. Those first couple weeks of training camp my rookie year were pretty rough. I just kept working hard."

Birk became one of the best centers of his generation, going to the Pro Bowl six times. Making as much of an impact off the field, Birk was the first Ravens player to win the NFL's Walter Payton Man of the Year award and was the first player in the league to show initiative when it comes to concussions and the effect on the body, donating his brain and spinal cord tissues after death to a Boston University medical school program.

Just 19 days after winning the Super Bowl, Birk announced his retirement on his own terms. He did so at a Baltimore elementary school, a nod to a reading program that reaches 100,000 children through his foundation.

NFL commissioner Roger Goodell congratulated Birk on a "great career on and off the field." Wide receiver Torrey Smith called him "one of the greatest people I've ever played with." Offensive tackle Michael Oher referred to Birk as the "best leader ever."

"It is a great way to end it," said Birk, who was 36 years old at the time of his retirement. "No one is entitled to a Super Bowl. But I'm so grateful and fortunate to be part of the team. It is a special team and the run that we made, the championship we won, is something I'll never forget."

Michael Oher

Michael Oher celebrated the Ravens' 2012 Super Bowl victory by enjoying the moment on the field with the Tuohy family.

It would have been the perfect ending to a movie, if one hadn't already been filmed. Oher's life was the subject of *The Blind Side*, a book-turned-blockbuster movie about an impoverished black child adopted by a wealthy white family and mentored to football stardom.

"Without them, I don't know if I'd be here or not," Oher said. "They took this road and made it easier on me."

While Oher embraces his adopted family, he wants to distance himself from the film that grossed $300 million and led to an Academy Award for Sandra Bullock.

Oher's not the "*Blind Side* guy," a nickname casual fans often call him. In fact, he played the entire postseason in 2012 at right tackle and *not* protecting Joe Flacco's blind side.

He also knew how to play football in high school, unlike the Big Mike character in the movie. He wasn't a lost soul who needed an on-field pep talk from Bullock. He hasn't even met Bullock.

Oher insists he wasn't as slow as the movie portrayed him. He wasn't as overweight or socially inadequate as what everyone saw on the screen.

This is why Oher has only seen the movie once.

"I'm tired of the movie," Oher said. "Football is what got me here, and the movie, it wasn't me."

The real Oher is the one who was drafted in the first round by the Ravens in 2009. The Ravens have always been able to count on Oher for his toughness and durability and consider him a throwback type of player. He has never missed a game in his career and became the first Ravens rookie offensive lineman since Jonathan Ogden in 1996 to start all 16 games.

While he has struggled in pass protection throughout his career, he didn't give up a sack on the playoffs. But none of the national media asked him about that during Super Bowl week, focusing instead on the Hollywood portrayal.

"I don't know how long that movie was, but 75, 80 percent wasn't who I am," Oher said. "It hit on some things, but the football part of it I didn't like. I always knew how to play football growing up. Personality-wise, it was way off. It's a movie; it's Hollywood."

Teammates and even coaches will use *The Blind Side* to rib Oher. The movie poster was hung in the locker room during his rookie season.

During the 2012 season, Ravens coach John Harbaugh wanted to stress the need for completed blocks. So, he showed the team the outrageous movie clip in which the Oher character blocks a high school opponent the length of the field and dumps him over a fence.

"Everybody laughed and fell on the floor," Oher said. "It was all fun."

Even though Oher would never go for a sequel, he couldn't deny that his championship journey seems like a Hollywood ending.

"[It] is unbelievable, knowing where I came from to going to the Super Bowl, somewhere you wanted to be all your life," he said. "It's remarkable."

Vonta Leach

Ask Vonta Leach about his favorite memory in the 2012 Super Bowl and he responds with a trivia question:

Who is the only fullback to touch the ball first and last for the championship team's offense?

Leach then flashes a smile and it's easy to figure out the answer. He caught an eight-yard pass from Joe Flacco on the Ravens' first offensive play and ran the ball for one yard on their last one.

"They were just throwing a dog a bone," Leach said in that good ol' country boy accent.

Not bad for someone who touched the ball just 30 times in the regular season that year. In between those rare moments with the ball, Leach nailed 49ers linebacker Patrick Willis or anyone else who got in his way during the Super Bowl.

Leach's job requires him to do the dirty work. His effectiveness is measured by running back Ray Rice's rushing totals and the number of times Joe Flacco doesn't get touched in the pocket. His old-school, no-nonsense approach to sticking his helmet into the chests of linebackers has earned him such nicknames as "The Hammer" and "The Coke Machine."

Leach is the best of what is a dying position in the NFL. Teams are using fullbacks less because they're spreading defenses out more these days. Plus, there are fewer players wanting to line up at fullback because of the demands of the position.

"It feels like you've gone through a train wreck," Leach said. "Sometimes I can't even get out of the bed, and I walk around real slow with a limp. People ask me, 'Why are you walking around like you got a limp or something?' and I tell them, 'No, my body is just trying to get back and adjusted.'"

Usually three days after the game, his body begins to recover, though this is a relative term. There are always aches and pains, a constant test to his toughness.

Leach's sacrifice isn't recognized in this Fantasy Football era, but it commands respect in the locker room. Rice has given him a television and a wristwatch. Flacco once bought him expensive speakers.

"Vonta is a fullback, the most under-recognized position in the game because of all the physical abuse he does to his body to see another man shine," Rice said. "The fullback position is not a pretty job. One thing about it is, Vonta wants that responsibility, to go out there and just knock people out for me to be successful. He's done it for many backs over the years. They all can vouch for him. Linebackers around the league know he's coming for you."

After the Ravens won the Super Bowl, Leach returned for a parade in his honor in Rowland, North Carolina, his hometown of 1,000 people. For years, there has been a sign that greeted motorists that read: "Home of Vonta Leach. NFL Player." Now, it can add: Super Bowl champion.

"When the confetti fell I was like, 'Oh my God.' It was the happiest moment of my life," Leach said. "I finally can say I'm the world champion."

Josh Bynes

Six months before making the biggest play of his life, linebacker Josh Bynes laid in a hospital bed with no idea whether his football career was over.

He was unable to turn his body to either side. There was a tingling sensation down his right leg. The pain was excruciating.

Doctors told Bynes that he had a broken back.

"I busted out crying after I heard that," Bynes said. "It was tough."

Tests revealed cracked vertebrae at the bottom of his spine. It's an injury that usually occurs in a car accident. Bynes suffered his on the practice field.

An awkward hit to Bynes' back while he was making a tackle in late July 2012 put the undrafted player's future, much less a spot on the roster that season, in jeopardy.

Surgery wasn't required. Time would eventually heal his back. Bynes returned six weeks later, only to get cut by the Ravens. He began the season on the practice squad.

The Ravens promoted Bynes to the active roster when they put Ray Lewis on injured reserve/designated for return six games into the season. He became a valuable member on special teams. It wasn't until the Super Bowl that everyone realized how valuable.

All the Ravens had to do was make one last tackle to hoist up the Lombardi Trophy. Ravens quarterback Joe Flacco was so concerned that his team's 34-31 lead wouldn't hold up that he talked to teammates about running onto the field to make the final stop.

Luckily for the Ravens, they had Bynes. 49ers returner Ted Ginn Jr. fielded the free kick at his own 18-yard line and accelerated close to midfield after breaking tackles from James Ihedigbo and Jimmy Smith.

That's when Bynes came from Ginn's side and wrapped his arms around him. He tossed Ginn to the turf right in front of the Ravens' sideline, which erupted in celebration.

Bynes got up from the tackle, threw his hands behind him, and let out a scream.

"I'm never going to forget that," Bynes said of his only tackle in the Super Bowl. "It may not be that big of a deal, but if that guy would've scored, it would've been a big deal then. That's something I'm always going to remember. That solidified the Super Bowl. That was it. Once I got him to the ground, that's over, it's a wrap, and I was just glad to be that person who made the last tackle."

In one season, Bynes had gone from the lowest point of his football career to the highest.

"Being the select few that actually gets the chance to play in the NFL—and being able to win the Super Bowl—that's the last goal of all the goals that there are in football," Bynes said. "That's why winning the Super Bowl is the best thing ever. You've got world-class athletes, guys winning MVPs, but no matter what it is they feel like their careers weren't complete because they didn't get to win a Super Bowl."

EPILOGUE

A year after celebrating a Super Bowl triumph, the Ravens were left with mixed feelings at the close of the 2013 season. There was disappointment from failing to make the playoffs, and there was determination to return to that standard of excellence.

"We understand that we didn't get the job done," coach John Harbaugh said, "and we understand that we've got to go to work to improve in every single way that we possibly can."

The Ravens' 2013 season wasn't a disaster, but it wasn't what the Ravens envisioned following their second Super Bowl title. The Ravens sputtered from the outset and never really recovered. Baltimore was 4-6 before going on a four-game winning streak and finished with lopsided losses to New England and Cincinnati to fall from playoff contention.

This was the first time in Harbaugh's six seasons as head coach that the Ravens missed the playoffs. It was also the first time that the team didn't finish with a winning record.

The Ravens' 8-8 mark didn't sit well with anyone in the organization.

"I think it's fair to say it's a failure because our goal is to be one of the top 12," owner Steve Bisciotti said. "There are bigger failures out there. There are teams that are a whole lot more disappointed. If we found ourselves at 3-13 like the Falcons, I think they're sitting there thinking we've got to make a lot of major changes, and I really don't think we do. If 8-8 is a failure, I hope it's a long time before I feel worse than this."

The Ravens are a victim of their own success. In 1999, coach Brian Billick's first season, an 8-8 season was lauded as a success. It says a lot about how the Ravens' franchise has grown when breaking even is considered an underachievement.

Under Harbaugh, the bar has been raised for a franchise that elevated itself among the likes of the New England Patriots, Green Bay Packers, and Pittsburgh Steelers. The Ravens' goal is to be one of the elites, contend every season, make the playoffs, and take their shot at another Super Bowl.

There are high hopes for the Ravens' offense, which relies on quarterback Joe Flacco throwing deep downfield to wide receiver Torrey Smith and over the middle to tight end Dennis Pitta. There is a tremendous amount of trust in their defense, which blends the veteran leadership of linebacker Terrell Suggs and defensive tackle Haloti Ngata with the promising upside of young defenders like cornerback Jimmy Smith and safety Matt Elam.

There is also the added motivation of falling short a year after sitting atop the football world.

"You learn more in failure than you ever will in success," Suggs said after the Ravens' season-ending loss in Cincinnati. "This is a crappy feeling. We're going to learn tremendously from it. You had better believe we're going to come into next season with a sense of urgency."